How to manage in
a flat world

FT Prentice Hall
FINANCIAL TIMES

In an increasingly competitive world, we believe it's quality of thinking that gives you the edge – an idea that opens new doors, a technique that solves a problem, or an insight that simply makes sense of it all. The more you know, the smarter and faster you can go.

That's why we work with the best minds in business and finance to bring cutting-edge thinking and best learning practice to a global market.

Under a range of leading imprints, including *Financial Times Prentice Hall*, we create world-class print publications and electronic products bringing our readers knowledge, skills and understanding, which can be applied whether studying or at work.

To find out more about Pearson Education publications, or tell us about the books you'd like to find, you can visit us at **www.pearsoned.co.uk**

PEARSON
Education

How to manage in a flat world

Get connected to your team – wherever they are

Susan Bloch and
Philip Whiteley

 Prentice Hall
FINANCIAL TIMES

An imprint of **Pearson Education**
Harlow, England • London • New York • Boston • San Francisco • Toronto • Sydney • Singapore • Hong Kong
Tokyo • Seoul • Taipei • New Delhi • Cape Town • Madrid • Mexico City • Amsterdam • Munich • Paris • Milan

PEARSON EDUCATION LIMITED

Edinburgh Gate
Harlow CM20 2JE
Tel: +44 (0)1279 623623
Fax: +44 (0)1279 431059
Website: www.pearsoned.co.uk

First published in Great Britain in 2007

ISBN 978-0-273-71245-9

British Library Cataloguing-in-Publication Data
A catalogue record for this book is available from the British Library

10 9 8 7 6 5 4 3 2 1
11 10 09 08 07

Typeset in 9.5/14.5pt stone serif by 30
Printed by Ashford Colour Press Ltd, Gosport

The publisher's policy is to use paper manufactured from sustainable forests.

Contents

part 2   ## The Individual

Foreword

Over the past few years, markets around the world have opened up in a way that no one could have imagined. Businesses now operate across multiple countries, which has important implications for those who work internationally, as well as for those who work locally. That means that every day and in many facets of our lives we are dealing with and connecting with many people who we may never meet face to face. The local mindset has become global whether we like it or not.

The world somehow seems flattest in Asia. In our business, we are sourcing from and working with people everywhere in the global village. We have got the elephants running, not dancing. This means dealing with unprecedented ambiguity and uncertainty that managers need to cope with every day. The ten strategies that have come to life from the research portrayed in this book will help us deal with all those complexities and paradoxes that the flat world brings with it.

Bijay Sahoo
Chief People Officer
Reliance Retail, India

Preface

The research

People love to read and learn from stories. In order to benefit and learn from business stories, we believe research needs to come from the interviews. Hence our framework while we were planning and then writing this book was to build on interviews and questionnaires and translate the research into strategies and key learning points. Our professional experience as, respectively, business coach and business journalist has enabled us to gather insights from 64 successful managers in a variety of roles and range of commercial sectors, with many different functional and educational backgrounds. Not only are they already working and thriving in the flat world, they are also engaging day-to-day with people who are from different religions, different cultures, often virtual strangers and in dispersed teams. They openly shared their experiences, passions, beliefs, and anxieties. Many acknowledged that this opportunity to articulate and think through some of the many issues they had been dealing with was an extremely useful exercise. Each of us in our own way can learn from their successes and struggles. It is clear that time for studied reflection seems to be a rare and valued commodity. We hope *How to Manage in a Flat World* will give you the time for just that.

In total, 25 managers from China, India, North America, Singapore, Western Europe, North and South America and South Africa were interviewed in depth. We also conducted an online survey with 40 executives from around the globe to gather data. Across the two surveys, we included people from numerous business sectors and company types: large multinationals as well as small firms and start-ups, in retail,

IT, telecoms, electronics, luxury branded goods, venture capital, manufacturing, professional services, construction, banking, media and engineering. Their views represent what is happening in companies as small as 30 employees to as large as two million. Their teams are as small as four to as large as 30,000. One team is composed of as many as 60 different nationalities; most swing between three and 30. Teams may operate in as many as 140 countries across the globe, others in as few as two or three. Some teams are located in one country with virtual offices in other parts of it, employing people from many different countries; they are in joint ventures or working closely with suppliers. A range of individuals, including senior executives at multinational firms but also several mid-level managers whose responsibilities nonetheless extend across many time zones and cultures, were selected. The surveys feature strategies of business leaders and other managers in the 'old' economies of North America and EMEA (Europe, Middle East and Africa) as well as the rising powers such as India and China.

In addition, we comprised an international team of two, based in the UK and India – with the attendant issues of time differences, use of communications media and infrequent face-to-face meetings. Further, between us, we have working experience in five continents.

This data was distilled into ten clear strategies, set out in Part 2, Chapter 8; and practical learning points (at the end of each chapter) to enhance effective leadership in our flat, global world. These provide real insight into the daily reality of leading, managing and working from everywhere and anywhere. They also provide a solid foundation for leadership development initiatives in organizations, and curriculum ideas for schools and universities, which prepare people to manage many of the new complexities that make our working lives so exciting.

Susan Bloch
Philip Whiteley
June 2007

Acknowledgements

This work was in many ways a collaborative effort, involving a virtual international team of over 70 people, based all over the globe in this flat world. This extended beyond the two authors – one of whom is based in India, one in the UK.

First of all, we would like to thank the 25 executives who freely gave of their time to be interviewed in depth, and who gave such full and frank observations. We would also like to thank the 40 individuals who gave such detailed responses to the online survey. This book is based on their views, insights, perceptions and experiences.

Many people helped arrange the interviews – in particular, we would like to thank Steve Bridge and Matthew Sweetapple at Sheppard Moscow; Cristina Fernandez and Angela Gonzalez at the Madrid office of Gavin Anderson; Bob and Sally Garratt; Olu Ajayi; and the staff at Cranfield University.

For advice we would like to thank Liz Credé, also of Sheppard Moscow, and Jennifer Fitzgerald. And very special thanks must go to all those at Maximvs Publishing who gave technical assistance on the online survey, especially Stephanie Street, Maria Davies and Kelly Stanley.

Thanks are due also to Liz Gooster, editor at Financial Times Prentice Hall, for crucial advice and insight, and ongoing assistance.

Especial thanks are due to Rose, for her support and counsel.

Allon and Shelley are always there, despite the fact we are all on different sides of the world: thanks for listening and understanding. And to Harry Chadwick, who as a young teenager already manages so effectively in our flat world, for his wonderful e-mails.

This book is dedicated to the memory of John Chadwick,
whose inspiration shines on, regardless.

Introduction

The bullet train and the mule

When you work in the interconnected economy, you are always switched on. The portable computer is at hand, the web will answer your queries and your colleagues and friends are just a few clicks away. So why do we sometimes feel disconnected? Is it the jet lag and the working hours? Or the desire to sit down and talk with someone, the old-fashioned way? Or the nagging feeling that we don't really know our objectives, or our far-flung colleagues, as well as we would like?

There are really two internets: the electronic one, and the human one. The first advances like a bullet train; the second, at the pace of a mule. It only took a couple of generations to go from the clunky first computer to open-source software, artificial intelligence and the web. These inventions transformed the global economy, and have combined explosively with the opening up of world markets following the almost complete collapse of communism. In the memorable imagery of the 2005 book, *The World is Flat*, by Thomas Friedman, the world has become 'flat' – a single, global economy with most of the world's businesses electronically connected.[1]

Progress on the human internet, by contrast, has been slow. Since before the computer was invented, we have known what makes for effective co-operation. Elton Mayo, in studies at the Hawthorne factory in Chicago, USA, in the 1930s, discovered that the most significant element in determining a group of people's effectiveness was the way in which they are treated and respected. And yet, 75 years on, the lesson is only fitfully implemented. The very subject is absent from many a board meeting, and is only touched upon in companies' annual reports. Rates of failure in organizational change programmes, especially mergers, remain stubbornly high. The consistent findings that failure lies in lack of a style of leadership that is based on effective communication and engagement, are just as stubbornly ignored. For every Southwest Airlines there is a Northwest; for every Toyota there is a Rover.

The way we lead and relate to our colleagues is just as important to the global company as the infrastructure. But the principles underlying these practices are not universally applied. In this book we will ask: are we equipped to manage teams that span continents? Can we maintain a work-life balance when communications technology is always on? And are we able to carry over learning on teamwork, motivation and communication from the pre-flat world into the new economy?

❝It is like having your head in the oven and your feet in the freezer.❞

Our in-depth interviews and research with managers and leaders in global businesses show successes, struggles and triumphs amid a constant battle for balance and sanity in a changing world. Many record the challenge of adjusting when markets and businesses change rapidly: 'It is like having your head in the oven and your feet in the freezer.' (Girish Paranjpe, President Finance Solutions of Wipro Technologies) They also record some remarkable achievements, that have helped us draw up some of the key tenets that help people to manage effectively in this new context.

What do we mean by the 'flat' world?

The world is flatter in two broad, closely linked, areas: first, economically, the opening up of markets since the end of the Cold War, the rise of internet trading, cheapness of travel, improving educational standards in developing countries and so on have caused a vast increase in the value of global trade, and transformed its nature. The giant nations – India, China, Russia and Brazil – have been industrializing rapidly, and are serious players in the world economy. In contrast with a 19th–20th century 'colonial' pattern of advanced economies and developing nations, the early 21st century consists of thriving regions of economic development, developed around clusters of specialist skills, that may be anywhere in the world.

The second aspect of 'flatness' is the change in corporations that both reflect and to some extent drive these globalizing trends. The monolithic corporation, with departments or 'silos', run by Europeans, Japanese or North Americans, is being replaced by a complex network of joint ventures, outsourcing relationships and global sourcing. In addition, there is the growth of informal networks. Some of the major breakthroughs in technology are not made in the R & D departments of major companies, but in networks. An example is the Linux operating system; originally developed by and for individuals, but now supported by technology multinationals such as IBM, Sun Microsystems and Hewlett-Packard. Another innovation is the Wikipedia online encyclopaedia, maintained by volunteers. Websites increasingly feature a high level of involvement by the consumer. There is a demand for services that are free and controllable. What is clear is that in this 'flat' world, we also mean flat structures that are less hierarchical. This demands that leaders and managers learn to work differently. Status and position, combined with autocratic, directive leadership, are not enough to get the job done.

Agenda for managing in the flat world

Most of us are now familiar with the 'flat' world: low-cost entry to market; rapid developments in computer power, community-developed software, global sourcing, international virtual teams. We have to acknowledge the asymmetric paces of development – the bullet train speed of IT development, compared with the sluggish development of teamwork and communication. This is not easy, when team members may be stretched across time zones, and rarely meet face-to-face. But there are ways to accelerate the pace of learning in how to collaborate as teams. This book contains practical ideas from executives of proven, effective ways of international and cross-cultural teamworking.

ff We have to acknowledge the asymmetric paces of development. JJ

It is still common for a company to say to a disparate set of individuals: 'You're responsible for this project, to this deadline; you don't have to meet any more. Talk to each other in English, as best you can.

Get on with it.' It never ceases to amaze how much still gets lost in translation! This is an approach that relies too much upon chance. By applying what is known about international teamworking, from successful real examples and from theory, we can lower the element of chance and begin to achieve more. Any international company can implement modern organizational structures and connect everyone up to the net. The truly great returns – the exponential growth rates – come when this is harnessed by great leadership and teamwork, as the stories in the following pages will demonstrate.

Most discussion of business, particularly at the strategic level, is dominated by talk of market positioning, technology and structure, with little or no reference to trust, energy, teamwork and motivation. Wouldn't it be interesting if a CEO was quoted in the newspaper saying something like: 'I'm concerned at the energy levels in our international team – there's not enough buzz', or: 'I put a lot of thought into putting that team together, and I spend a lot of time motivating them. The commitment is there now, and I expect the results to follow'?

Trust and motivation are not 'soft' matters

Sometimes, the approach to teamwork and motivation is worse than indifference. Often, and especially in popular culture, the very subject invites satire and scorn. Few business journalists can resist a swipe at self-development workshops, especially if there is an outdoors activity involved. It is easy to criticize pretentious or poorly handled workshops. What is more damaging to business is the pretence that you do not need to bother with things such as good communication, welfare, teamwork, trust and high levels of motivation.

The people we interviewed consistently informed us about the importance of trust in business relationships saying that with trust, you can be sure someone will do something when they say they will. What can be more businesslike than 'getting things done'? Trust and teamwork are not the soft matters that one may or may not attend to. They are the means by which services and products are delivered.

Those times spent socializing or gossiping with the team; that extra phone call to Christina or Dmitri working in a small group in a different country, simply to ask: 'How are you?' actually form a key part of making businesses work. If the LAN or the internet connections are running slowly or malfunctioning, we take it for granted that the IT support people come in and fix it. If the human connections are faltering, we need to take it just as seriously – indeed more so; after all, technology is designed and run by people, too. The electronic and human internets demand equal attention.

The very concept of 'teamwork' in business has come under fire: is it only applicable in sport? Is it just PR – a rosy description of the corporation mostly for inclusion in recruitment brochures? Turning the question around, however, how much can we achieve on our own? In an interdependent world, where inventions and service delivery are far too complex for a single individual, the answer is 'practically nothing'. One venture capitalist, Allon Bloch, who has brought many hi-tech start-ups to initial public offering or a similar milestone, told us: 'I have never seen a company succeed on one person's vision. It's usually three-to-four critical people . . . They interact online all the time. They are good team players. They meet often. They develop a culture.'

What is it like to live in the flat world?

Not all regions and countries are changing in the same way, or at the same rate, but there does appear to be some convergence towards open markets, internet connectivity, international trade and urban dwelling. Some countries – most notably China and India, but also other parts of Asia and South America – are industrializing rapidly. The 21st century is visibly transforming societies. In China, entirely new cities are being constructed, with populations rising from zero to one million or more in a few years. The Dongtan 'eco-city', being constructed alongside Shanghai, for example, will eventually cover around 8,800 hectares of hi-tech industries, leisure centres and housing, with a population of several million. Shanghai itself, until recently dominated by the bicycle as a means of transport, now hosts the world's first magnetic-levitation (maglev) train. The world's fastest, it has a top speed of around 500 km per hour. Similar transformations have occurred in Russia. In Moscow, as recently as 1992, there was scarcely a conventional shop or café as a westerner would recognize it, or an advertising billboard, in the centre of the city, and Muscovites dressed in a style similar to that of 1950s England. Now, Russia is powering ahead as a capitalist economy.

For those in 'older' industrialized countries, the changes are far less visible. Indeed, for many people who have grown up in western Europe and North America, remarkably little has changed in the past 30 years *on the surface*. Many neighbourhoods look roughly the same; maybe a new shopping centre here, a closed factory there. The means of transport are mostly the same and in a few cases actually slower. Entertainments are similar and often retrospective, with popular music artists looking to the 1960s and 1970s for inspiration. Some TV and radio presenters are presenting the same shows, to the same format, as in the 1980s or even, in a few cases, the 1970s. For many in the baby-boomer generation who, as children or young adults, marvelled at space exploration and supersonic travel, the extent of change has been disappointing. They were sold a futuristic concept of the 21st century that involved space travel, all-new conurbations and a lifestyle of leisure as technology took the strain. What has happened has been that the economic and ecological barriers to faster travel have been greater than expected. Instead of moving *people* faster, we have learned to move *information* faster. Some of the things that have changed have taken us by surprise; but so have many aspects that have stayed the same.

While in the west daily lives feel very similar, the way in which services are delivered, of course, has been radically transformed. Instant access to pricing has transformed the way in which many consumer markets operate, from package holidays to antiques trading. Moreover, the industrialization and liberalization of economies that either used to be communist, or otherwise heavily protected by tariffs, or were held back by economic underdevelopment, affect everyone, with the rise of outsourcing and global sourcing. In the early 1990s the communist, capitalist and underdeveloped worlds were, economically speaking, like three quite different planets. Now they are being fused together.

The pace is uneven. Although the modern corporation is less colonial in structure and in senior-management attitude than it might have been 20 years ago, we are probably still in the early stages of transition to genuinely meritocratic, diverse global organizations. In our interviews, we did hear a few comments reporting of exclusion based on nationality or gender, or that one had to be male and/or of the nationality of the parent group, to advance to the highest echelons of a company. One female individual says of a major international manufacturing company that she deals with: 'It is still difficult if you are not male, and not of the nationality of the parent group, to be treated as equal.'

Thina Siwendu, a commercial lawyer based in Durban, South Africa, observes: 'I recall not so long ago a colleague complaining in the mining sector that they seem more and more to be a branch of the London business, with most decisions being taken there. I suspect that we will be aware of the critical mass if we experience a rush by multinationals to invest here.' She adds, however, that some South African businesses are making progress: 'In the financial service sector, there seems to be emphasis by multinational finance houses to employ black Africans and allow them to lead the local business. Examples are Actis and JP Morgan. I would say that there the transformation is evenly balanced.'

How do we (should we) manage in a flat world?

The relative importance of teamwork, communication and motivation – of the human internet – is growing in the flat world. As communications become cheaper and more people and more economic regions are drawn into global trade, the economic barriers to trade have been dramatically reduced. Even the poorest regions, through micro-financing and the spread of mobile telephones, have started to become to be engaged in the world economy. There is global recruitment for talent, and global sourcing of goods and services. In this competitive environment, where access to the latest technology is not a preserve of a wealthy elite, the only distinguishing features of an organization are the skills, capability and motivation of the people who are hired.

❝ The only distinguishing features of an organization are the skills, capability and motivation of the people who are hired. ❞

Many business teams now stretch across the world, and for their members, the modern world's 'flatness' is not an abstract or future notion. It affects every moment of their working lives. Where five or ten years ago they would have been working in a large department with a clear hierarchy, or perhaps in a comfortable expatriate posting with colleagues mostly of similar background, now they are working in semi-permanent project teams, communicating mostly via the internet, with colleagues of similar level of authority, who are diverse in background. They are likely to be operating in many more countries, some of which are new to capitalism.

There is much literature on how the world has become 'flat'. There is plenty of discussion on why it is flatter, and how it has become so. Much of the focus is on the agenda for politicians and CEOs in shaping their strategies. There is less on what the radical changes mean for the people charged with making things work at an operational level. What do we need to do? How can we achieve our objectives, pursue our ambitions and maintain a personal life? Yes, we need to understand the changing world; but that isn't enough. There are implications for how we manage and conduct ourselves, as well as for what we know. There are challenges and complications with managing in a flatter world, as well as opportunities. What has emerged is a potentially irreconcilable conflict between the desire for structural leanness and the need for high levels of engagement and teamwork. Part of the flattening of the world has consisted of new media reaching out to and connecting with new, underdeveloped regions. But another aspect has seen virtual connections replacing more traditional forums such as the regional meeting. To what extent can, and should, this latter development go?

> **A potentially irreconcilable conflict between structural leanness and high levels of engagement and teamwork.**

Curbing costly, energy-consuming business travel is often openly encouraged, for example Lucy Kellaway, in her much-read Monday column for London's *Financial Times*, wrote on 7 August 2006: 'At a guess I would say that 90 per cent of business trips could be cancelled with no damage to the business. People travel on business because it makes them feel important, because they are paranoid that something bad will happen if they do not and because they want air miles that enable them to fly even more.'

This view, however, is strongly resisted by some of our interviewees. For them, regular face-to-face meetings of international teams are as essential a part of running an organization as being on the internet. They provide the trust, rapport and the teamwork that create great companies. They yield better innovations, and more robust organizations. They are not done to 'feel important'; quite the opposite – they are encouraged by leaders who want to understand their people and their markets and do not wish to hide in ivory towers. There is a fundamental conflict here, with no easy answers.

Miles Flint, Global President of Sony Ericsson Mobile Communications, told us: 'When I do market visits, they can mostly be done in two days. You cannot see how shops are laid out in Singapore unless you see it first hand; you can't get a sense of a customer without seeing them first hand. You cannot get a sense of the local team's morale without meeting with them formally or informally and they like to arrange press interviews during the visit if possible. None of this can be done remotely but generally the two days is enough. My predecessor said: "You will find that never do you *not* have jet lag."'

Effective virtual and face-to-face communications reinforce one another. Antonio Sedan, a manager at Colombia-based manufacturer Comai, told us: 'If we have good relationships and intense virtual communications, when we meet it is like an explosion of effusiveness that creates strong bonds for future virtual communications.'

This leaves some serious decisions that have to be made on how often people meet physically; also where (is it always the central office?); but most importantly: for what purpose? We will explore these matters, drawing on examples of effective teams.

Does culture matter?

Much literature on international teamworking focuses on culture, and more specifically upon cultural differences and how difficult it is for people of different cultures to work together. This has yielded useful clues as to some of our underlying attitudes to hierarchy, the organization and decision-making. But it has encouraged a propensity to national stereotyping that remains uncomfortably common in international teams. A wealth of empirical evidence has established universal values that everyone expects from work: the chance for achievement, affiliation and to be treated with respect. Some of the most effective managers we interviewed regarded cultural differences as superficial, and acknowledged a common humanity.

Achievements being made

Despite all the challenges of international and virtual working, some great work is done on teamwork and communication by managers and their teams. *How to Manage in a Flat World* describes some highly performing teams and draws out the lessons. We know more than we think we know. Above all, we need to integrate our efforts on teamwork, adaptiveness and communication with business planning –

“We need to integrate our efforts on teamwork, adaptiveness and communication with business planning.”

and some of the managers we interviewed have valuable advice on this – so that progress sticks and we don't experience another 75 years of institutional amnesia, forgetting and having to rediscover the importance of motivation. If we put as much thought and ingenuity into constructing the human internet as has been devoted to the electronic internet and the 'flat' global economy, the rewards will be:

- Higher levels of understanding about team goals and individuals' roles

- Higher engagement of team members

- Retention of talented individuals
- Greater awareness of the external environment
- Superior business returns
- Better relationships at work and at home.

The Team

1

'Flat' teams need direction

It doesn't happen by saying 'You are a team'.

Miles Flint: Global President, Sony Ericsson.

key points

- 'Flat', or low-hierarchy international business teams need conscious leadership and direction; this will not just 'happen'.

- You are more likely to succeed if you blend team-building with strategic and business planning meetings. It helps to have a higher concentration of face-to-face meetings at the start of an organizational transition or project.

- Trust and engagement are just as important in planning process and systems as in the creative industries.

- With outsourcing relationships and complex global customer interfaces, many teams cut across departmental and organizational boundaries as well as national ones.

- Great care needs to be devoted to planning meetings and communications in globally dispersed teams, to ensure clarity of vision and direction.

You have your 'flat' team. You've got your finite travel budget. Go ahead, lead. The first lesson you may learn is that a low-hierarchy international team does not sort itself; it requires leadership. But what does this mean in practice? The overarching themes emerging from our research are: integrate team dynamics and corporate goals to provide focus. Remember that if there is lack of clarity of direction, or lack of knowledge of the team's strengths and interests, this can affect how prepared they are to meet the stated mission, and how they fit into the larger organization.

Followership

This chapter looks at the challenge of creating *followership* as well as leadership within a geographically dispersed collection of often highly talented – and perhaps opinionated – individuals. People need to be aware of what a boss and colleagues on the other side of the world expect from them. This will require flexibility and good communication. Indeed, the imagery of 'flatness' in organizational hierarchies is well established. In the late 1980s, multinationals restructured and 'delayered', created open-plan offices and multi-site working groups. Today, most teams in international organizations are 'flat', based on meritocracy, possessing little or no formal hierarchy. There are also impermanent project teams, often with membership stretching across organizational boundaries. Teamwork has increased as people learn to work in matrix structures in an interdependent manner.

In addition, complexity in the sciences and product development, in particular, increasingly means that international teams from more than one organization are collaborating. This pattern extends to most industries. For example, early 2007 witnessed signals from the motor giants Toyota and Ford that they would be collaborating on areas of technological development. In January 2007, Toyota's president Katsuaki Watanabe told the *Nikkei Business Daily* that he would be willing to co-operate with the US car giant. This followed a meeting in December 2006 between Ford's CEO Alan Mulally and Toyota's chairman Fujio Cho. This development, unimaginable a couple of decades ago, is likely to become more common as the complexity and cost of research and development increase. In *The World is Flat*, Thomas Friedman highlights the push towards legal reform giving more freedom to permit cross-licensing, which will encourage yet more joint development work as organizations conclude that the creation of a complex product is beyond its capability on its own. He writes: 'The more your legal structure fosters cross-licensing and standards, the more collaborative innovation you will get. The PC is the product of a lot of cross-licensing between the company that had the patent on the cursor and the company that had the patent on the mouse and the screen.'[2]

❝The creation of a complex product is beyond its capability on its own.❞

Getting into focus

There is a strong tendency to push ahead with international communications, flat team structures and complex joint venture arrangements without fully attending to the teamwork and communication skills necessary to provide direction. Executives in a joint venture or merger typically spend 80 per cent of their time on financial negotiations and legal discussions, and only 20 per cent on post-deal integration and vision. This imbalance has caused many an acquisition or merger to fail to enhance business performance.

The latest KPMG study of large-scale mergers found the now common situation that only around one third add value to the shareholders (*The Morning After – Driving for Post-Deal Success*, KPMG 2006). In the detail of the study, more executives are waking up to the need to treat cultural and teamwork matters as being of equal importance to legal and regulatory concerns. The most favoured actions reported for the next deal were: plan earlier, perform additional cultural due diligence, and set up a dedicated team to handle post-deal work. Yet awareness is growing slowly; only a half of respondents had considered themselves well prepared for IT and reporting integration, and only one fifth for dealing with cultural issues. Earlier research by KPMG identified overwhelming evidence that organizations that paid considerable attention to the misleadingly titled 'soft' matters of teamwork and culture were far more likely to be successful (*Unlocking Shareholder Value*,

1999 and 2001). Later in this chapter a case study of a well-executed deal by Sony Ericsson is considered. The lesson does not only apply to mergers and joint ventures; it is likely to be a universal feature of leadership in the flat world.

Slowness in applying findings from people-management related research was noted in the Introduction. It means that many managers are plunged into an exciting but underprepared situation where complex teams have challenging tasks and may or may not constitute a strongly communicating network that gels. They have only a vague idea of 'where they are going', and how they will get there.

Leading out of the darkness of ambiguity

Many of the executives we spoke with describe the ambiguity of a 'flat' team, where there may be little formal hierarchy and challenges with international communications. It can create a feeling of being in the dark. So how can leaders create light?

One way is to end the segregation of business planning from individual and team development. This is true of all business teams, but especially crucial in international teams, where face-to-face time is limited and must be used to its best advantage, and where difficulties in team interaction can create an exaggerated impact on the bottom line, owing to the sheer difficulty of repairing fractured relationships that are stretched across the globe.

Segregating strategic and other commercial considerations from team-work is common but illogical, and our research yielded some practical ideas on how to overcome this. Many executives have experience of strategic processes that involve sitting through tedious PowerPoint presentations. When personal development and team-building activities are not embedded in the organizational goals, they are viewed as a waste of time by many; they may seem frivolous, often involving outdoor activities with no direct link brought to bear from the learning they provide to their challenges.

Blending business meetings with team-building work and 'time to hang out together' is highly beneficial to all parties. It makes the business side more engaging, and the social interaction and teamwork more purposeful. For international teams, there is limited time to meet. This has the disadvantage of allowing less time together than the team might ideally need, but it does carry with it an advantage in that time spent together is precious, creating an impetus to use it well. It can also help to clearly delineate strategic and socializing time (face-to-face) from day-to-day interactions, which can be done through other media. When managed well, fire-fighting is displaced by a strong dashboard, clear milestones, and a highway to drive on.

Concetta Lanciaux, Executive Vice-President Synergies at LVMH, finds the blending of individual and team agendas into the corporate agenda very effective. She says: 'It is essential that teams bond. Professional activities are bonding events just as much as a social event. Our LVMH House sessions normally last a couple of days during which there is formal and informal interaction where people get the chance to ask the difficult questions and discuss solutions and options to the way forward. People are not motivated if you get together *only* to socialize. However, combining the two is very successful. After the workshop participants fill out evaluations where they usually say that they appreciate the blend of the content, the networking and the sharing of knowledge.'

In management-speak, this agenda is normally addressed under the term 'alignment'. People talk of having human resources strategies aligned with business strategies; which is laudable, but not enough. The problem with this terminology is that it is rather impersonal and passive, not addressing the energy and motivation that generate truly great results. It may not enough to be 'aligned'. We need also to address matters such as understanding, direction and energy.

David Grigson, CFO of Reuters, comments: 'I would want to have more face-to-face communication with them [my team]. I would want more face-to-face contact; more time spent discussing their issues and concerns. Managing your people is always less urgent, but always more important.'

Above all, this is a business consideration, not just a personal one – there are heightened risks by neglecting the team. These include, says David: 'Lack of motivation; a sense of not being fully recognized or appreciated; when a good job gets done it is not always possible to appreciate just how hard it was. I think good working relationships are based on a fundamental understanding of what people are doing and how they are feeling. Without that [time spent meeting] being formally in the diary, the risk is that there are long periods go by when there is no contact. I do my best to spend time away from my desk walking the floors here in London. I make as much time for social interaction as I possibly can but it never feels enough. It's good to be seen wandering around, saying "Hi", taking an interest.'

In addition, Jacob Aizikowitz, CEO of US-Israeli firm XMPie, says: 'Twice a year we have management meetings off-site. We take all the management to a place for two days, to discuss long-term issues, including strategy. Sometimes we invite a guest speaker. It will be held in New York or Israel, but not in the office. We may spend half a day doing something that's more fun; for example when we were in Israel we went to a golf course and took lessons in golf. When we were in up-state New York – two hours out of the city – we did some kayaking. Things of that nature.'

He adds that phone conference conversations are necessarily limited to immediate practical concerns, but this misses important matters that must be catered for elsewhere. 'I think it's simply the case that when the team is dispersed, and connected by other forms of communication, really there is no option except for discussing the subject matter; you're always meeting in a limited amount of time. I believe that when we meet face-to-face strategic discussions are also important. They might not be strategic – they might concern how something is working in the company, but no one has talked about it or called a meeting about it. But when discussing, socializing, it may come up.'

Behind the scenes: teams in synch with the business

Many teams find it helpful to arrange a higher-than-usual frequency of face-to-face meetings at the start of a project, or in a new phase, such as post-merger or reorganization. This can create the bedrock of trust and strong relationships that help sustain virtual communications. But the face-to-face meetings have to be well used, with a sense of purpose.

Sony Ericsson is the result of a cross-cultural tie-up between Swedish and Japanese companies. There are major R & D centres in Sweden, Japan, China and the USA, and manufacturing in China, Malaysia, Mexico, Brazil, Japan and France. There are seven sales areas: North America, South America, Western Europe, the countries of the Commonwealth of Independent States, the Middle East and Africa, Asia-Pacific and Japan.

Miles Flint is Global President, having joined in 2004, two and a half years into the joint venture. When he joined, the organization was going through a difficult patch. He was faced with the task of aligning managers from different companies, and many different cultures. His recent results show that his approach has worked.[3] He has overseen, as we discussed earlier, a blending of personal and team development with business planning. There is also a marrying of such initiatives to the phase of development of a young company. 'When I joined, I got a sense that we had been in turn-around mode, but there was the next stage to get people to: about working more effectively, building trust and common understanding; just getting people together.'

❝Working more effectively, building trust and common understanding.❞

'They have to spend time together: eat together, relax together, before they will begin to say: "This is the same problem in Japan as the guy in France had" and work together. It doesn't happen by saying: "You are a team". The "24 team" – of senior leaders in the business – went away to Denmark for "impact-type" work. There was a lot of scepticism. I was sceptical. I didn't really understand what we could learn on an outward-bound course. But it was mixed with a lot of focus on the business. That group gets together three times a year. The very first one I did in the mid-1990s was three days: pure orienteering and abseiling, then we tackled a couple of business issues; tried to integrate business issues into the teamwork exercises. There are things you can do in an hour that are fun and can bring a sense of achievement, rather than spend a whole day.'

Prior to this investment in team-building, there had been considerable work done in building the vision at the start of the joint venture, 'with McKinsey in a basement in Ericsson's headquarters in London', he says. This planned integration of people and cultures, with considered interventions to support organizational development at each stage of a new joint venture or merger, is by no means universal practice, as we noted earlier. Miles identifies some of the dynamics that are inevitable in such a tie-up that the programme has addressed: 'Where you have a joint venture or an acquisition, there is a tendency to feel, "The way we do things is better", and you can have a lot of rivalry and jealousy. But here people recognized the inherent strengths that they brought respectively. The individual companies fitted together well. Many joint ventures are essentially companies forced together by difficult business situations. If you have [teams or groups of] people who each think they have the best car design process it can be very difficult to rationalize. There was a little bit of that with Sony Ericsson – the company was losing money. The Sony Munich R & D centre was closed, and for the first two years there was a little bit of "winners and losers", making sure "my unit stays alive". This is said perhaps with the benefit of hindsight as I didn't come in until two years later. The other thing that I identify is that a lot of time was spent developing the mission, the vision, the ambition of what Sony Ericsson could be. This has paid huge dividends over time. Very early on, there was a dream of what Sony Ericsson could be.

'There was always a very strong feeling about potential; the concept of creating a new entity. It was a very, very tough situation. Ericsson was in a lot of difficulty; statements were made that unless you get this [business] profitable quickly you may have to close it down. On the other hand, there was a passion and commitment that carried the business through. There was a very passionate group of people in the company.'

Of the company now, he says: 'I think the culture [of Sony Ericsson] is identifiable. It is inherited from both parents, but identifiable. It is different from both, like a teenager: your parents are always your parents but as you grow up you develop your own personality. There is a passion and a commitment to the company. People feel that very strongly – in many cases they identify with that more strongly than with the parent that they come from. Many people look back at their time with one of the parents very positively, but have moved on to something that is new.'

One turn-around situation over a similar time period was encountered at healthcare products manufacturer SSL in Europe, which has restored its fortunes after a rough period in the early 2000s. Ian Adamson, European MD, has put a huge emphasis upon travelling and face-to-face meeting. 'One of the most important parts was not the formal aspect, but the informal; walking the floors, talking to people, talking to the right people, making sure that in every department, in every team you have someone sharing the vision and able to carry on the message. We increased the frequency of meetings, increased team briefings; became far more transparent, so that once every six months, at least, there was an overview of the group's performance and results. There would be Q & A sessions. I would hold regular three-monthly briefing sessions with most departments: give a brief presentation. An open and honest Q & A session gave a feeling of much greater transparency. People were encouraged to voice opinions, ideas; they were listened to. This openness and transparency certainly helped on the road to recovery.'

Unity of focus in complex teams

The 'flat', interdependent global economy is complex. There may be a multitude of teams criss-crossing organizational boundaries. This is not only the case in research for new product development, but will also occur with joint ventures, in-sourcing and outsourcing arrangements. For example, major software service providers will have individuals from the provider on location with the client for extended periods of time. The organizational identity can become blurred: who are they actually working for? For a manager of such a team, co-ordination and leadership can be tricky. Conor Gallagher is Head of Consulting Practice for financials and human resources at Germany-based software giant SAP, covering the UK and Ireland. There are 50 people in his team, many of whom are on site with the client for extended periods of time, meaning the team is 'remote' or 'virtual' in an organizational sense, as well as in terms of geography.

❝The organizational identity can become blurred: who are they actually working for?❞

Conor says: 'Being here as manager, it's a difficult one: how do you recruit and develop and retain the best people you can get your hands on, while rarely seeing them? They often have more contact with project managers at the client than with their [SAP] manager. You need regular, timely, detailed communication with one another, one-to-one.

'People are on-site on projects; they have a relationship with colleagues on the projects. Often, they adapt and "go native". One consultant has been seven and a half years with a client. In some cases they end up leaving us to work for the client. That's a huge loss to us.

'We work in areas that require a deep level of expertise; high complexity areas. There may be only one or two people going in for three months [so] there isn't a strong SAP presence locally. There isn't even always someone to go for a beer with. A major bank will want someone to lead up the e-recruitment solution. They can find themselves the only SAP person. These people are fairly autonomous, robust, resilient individuals; you often don't hear about their concerns – at least, until they leave. I have had eight people leave in as many months, and the exclusive reason for that was work-life balance. They don't want to be away from their family. When they were 26 it was fine; now they're 33, 34 and married with two kids; it's different. When they were 26 they would go out on the razz all the time and it was great fun. If people are going to leave, I would rather know about it in advance. There may not be a huge amount I can do – maybe transfer to product support roles; but our people must be geographically mobile. It's a challenge.'

This dual sense of remoteness – both geographically and in terms of organizational affiliation – is a common experience in a globalized economy with numerous joint ventures, alliances and long-term project work. Conor Gallagher puts effort – even if it

￼￼This dual sense of remoteness is a common experience in a globalized economy.￼￼

feels like excessive effort – into communication, in part to quell any misleading impressions before they can grow. 'Recently, four senior managers left from the executive board. There was a message from the central communications team; but that isn't adequate, you have to follow that up with a briefing to the team through a tele-conference. You have to socialize it for them and let them ask questions. There might be no response – they might say: "These guys change every three years and there'll be no difference" – which was the response in this case.'

Conor insists on meetings, even if they may appear to be inconvenient to all concerned, and with a heavy cost to the bottom line. 'Often it's just an opportunity for people to spend a day together, have a coffee and a lunch; reacquaint themselves with each other, discover who are the joiners and leavers. My view is that without it you start having a bunch of people who don't know each other. You wouldn't go any length of time without meeting your partner, or your friend. To sustain a relationship you have to have some engagement with your team; to understand who the 50 people are; what their personal ambitions are; their skills, as well as all about the project work and where it's going to be located.'

It can hit the bottom line in the short-term, so there needs to be an organizational commitment – but this is often handsomely repaid through higher engagement and lower turnover of people with key skills. Conor adds: 'You can't have effective conference calls if you are not [also] seeing people face-to-face as well. Ideally, you get people in a room together to get that dialogue going, but because of the type of people involved – that is to say, on fee-earning assignments – it is difficult to get them in the same place at one time. I have targets to hit. If I have 30 consultants in a room for a day that's costing me £1,500 × 30 or £45,000 (approximately $90,000). 'But it's very effective.'

Internally within organizations, team membership can be multiple, with competing demands. David Grigson, CFO of Reuters, comments: 'One of the issues for the finance function is that a lot of us operate in two teams. This especially applies to business support people who are part of the finance function but spend most of their time with the business operational guys. I encourage them to feel really connected to that part of the business they support, as that's the team through which they will add most value. They come to the finance table to ensure that they are adequately resourced and to take full advantage of the technical and other skills available within the function. To make sure we operate as "One Finance" across the group we run regular functional workshops that are intended to ensure we work together to form the high-performing team that is capable of delivering the decision support, risk management and robust controls that Reuters requires of us – and all at an industry leading cost.'

---

case study

Coca-Cola: RIP the departmental 'silo'

Even within large corporations team structures are becoming more complex, with increasing cross-departmental working. All multinational corporations like to celebrate the extent to which they break down silos (conventional internal business departments). It isn't just spin; there really is a need for more cross-disciplinary co-operation. It is no longer enough for the finance, marketing or HR department to deliver traditional services efficiently; they need to be working closely with business leaders, in a variety of semi-permanent teams. They need to understand the customers and the line managers; know which way the business and the markets are going and be members of project teams.

Cynthia McCague, Senior Vice President Human Resources at Coca-Cola, says: 'Ultimately, the objective of our team is playing an active part in the role of partnering with business leaders. Before I took this role, I spent six years leading the HR team for one of the largest Coke bottlers, across Eastern and Central Europe. We learned to operate based in a number of different countries. In the early 1990s, I was managing Coke's European HR function, but based in Atlanta, but living on a plane. In the last 15 years I have continuously led teams that were spread all over the place; not co-located. In today's competitive world, it's critical to put every bit of resource you have got – time, money, intellectual capital – all of that – directly into driving growth; any wasted resource of any kind is not helping you be competitive. You cannot afford luxuries any more. The function can and must play a real partnership role with our operating leaders to drive toward sustainable growth.

'We are adding value very directly in building capabilities that are necessary to ensure growth for this business. It is tangible: we have got to have the people and the overall capabilities (including process, environment) to be able to deliver what the business needs; whether that is an innovation pipeline or great consumer marketing. Our secret formula for this business is the inspiration of our people. Our people love working for and with our brands. Our job is to help leaders unleash that passion, that inspiration.

'Another new role for the HR function is to facilitate fast change – that's a direct role of the HR function; as well as building the culture, with our leaders. I fundamentally believe the primary role of HR is to deliver a workforce that's capable of continuously winning. That can be broken down into tangible metrics. We run the HR function as a business on a global basis. We aim to have the right resources, the right people, and the right cost structure. Another unique value-add is to focus on our significant spend on people, training investment and benefits, and for us to help management manage that expenditure like a business.'

Like many functions that have broken out of the 'silo' to become business partners, the human resources function for Coca-Cola tries to retain a sense of a team, and grapples with many of the challenges that others face when the members stretch across the globe: 'We have tried hard to steward resources by not flying around the world all the time, but two to three times a year we do come together: for operational reviews; for our own people development forum; development of vision, and actions to bring that to life. We've tried video-conferencing, and it's OK, but we now have enough of a platform to do very deep work through tele-conferences. You assume someone's in pyjamas; for someone else it's the beginning of the day.'

Clusters

Economically the world is increasingly dividing itself up into specialist clusters of skills, so any organization with global ambitions will rarely find the best skills for each discipline in the same country. A start-up from a smaller country will quickly have to market itself in different regions, as well as source talent globally, as it will not be able to satisfy its ambitions in the limited home market. The young technology firm XMPie, which provides publishing software for personalized marketing, has two locations straddling different continents, even though it only employs around 70 people. CEO Jacob Aizikowitz, responding to the question of why his firm is based in both Israel and New York, despite the time difference and other practical difficulties, admits: 'That's a very good question.' He adds: 'XMPie could have been in one location, but one of the realities when creating companies in Israel is that while you have very strong R & D skills in Israel, the markets are typically somewhere outside of Israel . . . when you start a company you also want to have a US company. That might be a financially driven decision. There's a perception that the main market is the USA. Investors wanted me in the main market. We're now spending a lot of time in the USA. Israel is an extremely small market; you cannot do enough business there.' From this platform, the company is now moving into the Asia-Pacific region. The same logic has driven many export-orientated firms in other small countries such as Iceland, Ireland, Belgium and Taiwan.

A few years ago, it would have been difficult to predict the spectacular growth in outsourcing that has meant that even back-office services like invoicing are delivered by specialist providers on the other side of the globe. Organizations providing complex services like software development or support to corporate clients have employees based semi-permanently with the client, creating ambiguity as to which organization they 'belong' to, who they report to and in which direction they are going.

> **❝ Inspirational communication has become as important as operational communication in setting direction. ❞**

So both communication technology and business developments are stretching teams around the globe. All of these evolutions mean that the way leaders lead has to change. Simply producing directive edicts is no longer enough. Inspirational communication has become as important as operational communication in setting direction.

Shell Retail: huge workforce in a dispersed operation

Shell Retail has an unusual structure in that only a small proportion of its total workforce are direct employees; the rest are employed by franchisees. It has arguably the most dispersed, and the most global, workforce of any enterprise (indeed it is worth noting that, for some companies, globalization has been around for a century). Leslie Van de Walle, President Shell Retail (at the time of interview; since appointed CEO of Rexam), found that the most effective way to lead such an organization was to have a tightly bound central management group. He has invested considerable management time in making sure that the principal management group – itself geographically dispersed – functions well as a team. The executive team consists of one Brazilian, one US American, one French person (Leslie Van de Walle himself), one Australian, one Filipino, one Austrian, one South African and the rest, British.

Leslie has overseen a transition from regional-based structure to a global one. 'We operate in between 120 to 150 countries, depending on what you define as a country – for example, whether a group of four small islands counts as one or four, so we are in almost every country apart from where governments don't allow us. Our turnover is £70 billion, 30 per cent of which is paid in tax. There are 45,000 fuel sites in the world, and about 30,000 shops. In terms of staff, we only have around 4,000 people directly employed; then there are 10,000 dealers or individuals running the sites; some of them own the site, some of them lease, some only operate. And there are between 800,000 and 1 million site staff.

'It is an interesting challenge when you look at the challenge of communication. You are covering the world. And you have a very small number of people that you are really driving. We have about 600 people in marketing; 300 people doing the network plan; choosing the sites; constructing the sites. Around 100 people doing strategy; 100 people implementing projects and the rest would be in sales and operations, running the dealers, dealing with customers. Then there are the support functions; finance, HR, and so on.'

The executive team is a team of ten people: five of them from the five regions; the other five from operational groups – marketing, networks, finance, HR and strategy. Out of the ten, four are based in London, the others are dispersed. One is in Brazil, one in Germany, one in the Philippines, one in Cape Town, South Africa, one in the USA.

▶

Globalization increased the need for teamwork at the most senior level of the organization, he found. A single global structure replaces one based on regions and functional departments within those regions. This leads to greater multidisciplinary co-operation, and the need for a shared vision as well as standardization and simplification of processes. 'I decided a high-performing team should work as a team,' Leslie says. 'Everyone is interdependent on each other. Sales need to have a marketing plan to work for them; marketing are not going to be effective if there are no salespeople to implement their plans – these would just stay in the box. We put a global organization together from the regions. We spent time building the vision, in order to establish a common sense of purpose: to be the best fuel retailer.'

Leslie put particular emphasis on face-to-face meetings in the crucial development phase of the new team. This is a recurring theme from our research: the bonding and shared understanding from well-structured face-to-face meetings and conversations provides the bedrock for successful virtual communications. It can be highly effective to have more face-to-face meetings at the start of a major project, or when teams are new for other reasons, then reduce the frequency later. 'We started in April 2004; finished by December 2004. We held a meeting a month; half of them on strategy – getting the team to own my vision. In 2005, we met for two to three days, once a month,' he says. He acknowledges that this represents a lot of time in meetings. But he adds: 'If you are leading a big business, working as a team, you have to make every single decision work globally; my way of doing it takes time. We now meet six times a year for one or two days. I think we're good at it; our ability to get motivated people from face-to-face meetings. If you have 100 countries, and you have ten [country representatives] meeting once a month, you cover the globe. It's not as much travelling as you would think if it's well organized. Nevertheless the biggest problem of working virtually is lack of communication. We underestimate that, especially in middle management.'

He tried to be as democratic and 'global' as possible. 'I was trying to be very careful, representing different parts of the business and give a chance to all. But life is unfair; we are a UK-based business. There were a disproportionate number of meetings in the UK, though I made sure that there were some in all locations. There is a trade-off between visibility and efficiency.'

With a reduced number of face-to-face meetings, now that the new teams and structure are embedded, there is considerable emphasis upon other forms of communication. 'That's something I have planned. It is leading-edge technology. What we do, for instance, is: we had the vision; the way of working, and we're cascading the vision. I have created an extended global retail leadership team – the direct reports to my direct reports. It's an elite group, that meets once a year. Once a quarter we have a webcast where we can discuss the results in detail, and they can discuss anything they want confidentially. A duty for them is to use that different treatment, and cascade the message down. For example, I cascade it to them; then they communicate to their people. You have more interest in what directly affects your business, than in what the boss of your boss says.

> **There is a trade-off between visibility and efficiency.**

Travelling does help. Face-to-face meetings are used to arrange highly interactive meetings, such as Q & A sessions, where staff, including junior staff, can quiz the managers. Sometimes the Q & A may last a full day. The aim is to convert global messages and objectives into local plans, owned by the local team. 'For example, the development plans; there's a Filipino expression of the global plans and suddenly it becomes theirs. It's very powerful; showing them what they do, but using their words.'

He also does a major video on the web – 10 to 12 minute video; state of the nation. Teams with extraordinary results are recognized on the website. Shell reports that of the 4,000 members of staff, 2,400 on average open the video every month. 'That has been very powerful in terms of managing morale, conveying results; and in terms of recognition,' Leslie says.

'I present awards also. All the winners come to an annual meeting; represent their group. It's a way for me to get the message down. The fact that they go there – everyone in the company knows; when they come back people ask them: "How was it?" The strong vision was communicated with the top 40. We have done benchmarking in terms of communication and the message is incredibly consistent. They know the vision – to be the best fuel retailer.'

This inspirational example shows how strong leadership can create bonding and clear direction even with extreme dispersal and the additional complexities of franchisees.

Do we all have to 'bond'?

One of the misconceptions that can arise when dealing with the human internet is that it always involves a time-consuming exercise in getting to know everyone you work with, and understanding what makes them tick. In the fast-moving 'flat' world where things have to get done and markets change quickly, it can appear to be a luxury. And indeed some people-development workshops can be excessive to the need that presents itself.

One US-based internet retailer comments: 'We buy and sell things online. Every minute that something goes wrong it's lost revenue. We need to be able to be nimble, and make decisions very fast. If the website in the UK is down, you cannot say: "Let's wait until tomorrow morning to discuss the issues." Likewise, if competitors lower prices. We make decisions within the hour. We also do long-range planning – we try to plan 15 months ahead.' But this company still invests in relationships, and in ensuring trust; after all, you cannot be nimble and responsive as an organization without a high degree of co-operation and understanding.

The fact that we need to have effective working relationships with the people we deal with does not mean that they all have to be equally close. You don't need to have a deep level of rapport and understanding with the people who provide your stationery; but you probably do need to have a closer level of understanding of direction with the people who provide more complex, business-critical functions like IT. And with colleagues with whom you are required to work closely, the relationship needs to be even more interconnected. Andy Warrender, leader of the fabrics division at Gore-Tex manufacturer Gore, works closely with his co-leader Rudi Kleis. He says of the relationship: 'If Rudi says he will do something, I know he will either do it or die trying.'

" If Rudi says he will do something, I know he will either do it or die trying. "

It is not always a case of maximizing the bond of mutual understanding, but having the appropriate level. There are times when a close relationship is a negative: sometimes an independent, objective judgement on cost-benefit analysis would be clouded if it were to be made by someone who is a close friend, and is set to gain or lose from the decision. The case study of United Biscuits (p. 22) includes an example of how an outsource provider can bring a more dispassionate assessment of costs and benefits on procurement. However, this example also illustrated the fundamental role of trust in all business operations.

An exaggerated emphasis on separation has appeared in corporate governance, where recent codes have arguably overemphasized the separation of non-executive directors, known as independent directors in the US, from the executive team. Separation and clarity of role should not mean hostility and suspicion. Indeed, while they include some necessary reform in limiting conflicts of interest, corporate governance rules represent a classic case study in ignoring the human internet.

> **"Separation and clarity of role should not mean hostility and suspicion.""**

What matters in your relationships with your chairperson, stationery supplier or purchasing department, is trust. They aren't all going to be equally easy to manage, but you do have to trust them. This is just as true in globalized supply chains and online trading. One of the key breakthroughs in internet retailing has been the practice of generating supplier and customer ratings on sites like eBay. Internet retailing may seem technical and impersonal, but in fact it is fuelled by emotion and judgement. Do you trust this person to pay you? If so, on what yardstick? Do we feel that this yardstick will continue to be reliable?

So we don't all have to 'bond', and it may not be necessary or desirable to get the whole team together for three days to talk about their personal histories, dreams and aspirations. On occasion, however, it will be. Managers putting teams together have to pay as much consideration to this judgement as to the technology and business structures that provide no more than the framework.

There can also be a temptation to say: 'This soft stuff about teamwork and bonding only matters in the creative industries like advertising or design or a dotcom start-up. It doesn't apply in our business – we're supply chain experts delivering widgets – all that matters is having the latest technology and a lean structure.'

It is common for managers and theorists to segregate companies into 'people-based' companies – like consultancies and investment banks – and 'process-based' companies like supermarkets and auto manufacturers. This may be a useful shorthand in some contexts, but in the final analysis all businesses are people businesses. Some of them have to run very efficient processes, but these are still managed by people, and trust always matters. Some of the most efficient processes in the business world are run by Toyota and Southwest Airlines, companies that invest enormously in recruitment, people development and teamwork. A supply chain is a link of relationships based upon technical skills and upon trust, that is supported by technology. Too often it's approached the other way around.

❝In the final analysis all businesses are people businesses.❞

---

case study

United Biscuits

Let's take one of the most traditional businesses that supplies retailers principally in the 'old' economy (long-established, factory-based production), where process efficiency is of paramount importance. United Biscuits is market leader or number two in most of Europe. Some of the brands are well established. McVities biscuits have had pretty much the same ingredients, packaging and logo since their introduction in 1925.

The west London-based multinational centralized its procurement processes to achieve economies of scale, deploying the latest technology, and contracted with a specialist procurement outsource provider, Xchanging. This is a typical 'flat world' reform for a multinational company: working across borders, and using economies of scale and a specialist outsource provider. But it also developed teamwork to bring about the change, paying just as much attention to the human internet as to the technology and structure. This was key to ensuring that the more logical procurement processes being introduced would bed down, be accepted and deliver cost savings. David Baker, Financial Controller Corporate Services at United Biscuits, has been responsible for the financial management of the new procurement system, in particular charged with ensuring that cost savings are 'captured' by the group, and not lost locally. Potentially, the approach could jeopardize existing relationships, for if head office is seen as coming to the regional centres to cut costs and impose a new, uniform process, this could prompt resistance. Experience suggests that this has been a common mistake with business process re-engineering projects.[4]

Like Concetta Lanciaux of LVMH, David has found that preparation should involve a blend of business planning with team bonding. 'I held a workshop in Barcelona, which is a nice place. The people who went there felt valued and treated well. It took them out of the working environment. We didn't even go to the Spanish office; we booked a hotel. We didn't want to get distracted by what was going on. It was a nice hotel – people came the night before, we organized a meal at a nice restaurant. The following day there were break-out rooms, and we spent some good quality time looking at the issues. We did the typical things to help people get to know each other. We wanted to get out of UB, and get into some of the motivations of people. We have also tried to incorporate the company that we have outsourced with, Xchanging. We invited them along to Spain, and sat down and talked about the issues, and about getting consistency. I don't believe that without face-to-face contact you can get the teamwork you need in order to manage effectively. Tele-conferences are not the same as being able to look into someone's eyes – then you can tell whether they buy in to what you are saying. We do have an email system with joint distribution lists so that everyone's copied in. We plan in the same way, with the same categories for each country.'

'You have the potential issue around trust involved in people at the centre coming in and saying: "This is a great idea", then you also have the added dimension of a third party. We didn't make people redundant, but over time we reduced the size of the [procurement] team. But in Northern Europe one person did do goods and services procurement. We looked into it and found that there was a lot more purchasing by the individuals at factory sites. These people weren't procurement experts. Because they weren't procurement experts, there was no consistency in suppliers, and no leveraging of the size of UB. Obviously, there were great opportunities. We were concerned [about this] but culturally the difference was that in France particularly, and Belgium to an extent, the management in factories had relationships with suppliers, and had done so for a number of years and had quite good deals, but of course didn't know what was available with pan-European deals. So they had this semi-procurement role that wasn't in their job descriptions.'

▶

This needed a sensitive approach. How was it tackled? 'With some difficulty. There was a double phase to it: first of all convince them that doing procurement consistently in different countries was a good idea. Having convinced them, the next issue was: whose model are you going to pick? An advantage of outsourcing is that you can pick something that is different to another person within the company.'

But, David adds: 'There were a lot of arguments: where do we need to be consistent? France, Holland and Belgium are different. I had done this kind of exercise before and everyone says: "We're different". But if you have a strong process, the process and quality should be able to cope with the vagaries of one particular area. It has taken a lot longer than we would have liked.'

'If you start going in and telling people how to do things, it doesn't work. You have to respect people. They may well be doing a good job; you can't go in and assume that they're doing a poor job – the first thing they will do is find examples where they could do it cheaper. This is a massive project; there are massive savings. There are probably instances where people could outsource and could get a better price [but it would take] x number of hours. The trouble is, if you get their backs up, they go onto the internet and try to prove you wrong. This is non-productive time.'

'In Northern Europe, we pulled all the people together in a hotel. The Managing Director of Northern Europe went round the team; anyone could put their hands up to volunteer if they could find extra savings; but with one caveat – no extra staff. We employ people to make biscuits, not become procurement experts. If you have a personal interest in something succeeding, you're far less able to be objective than procurement people, who can take it or leave it. They have detachment, and that is an advantage of an outsource team.'

> **❝They have detachment, and that is an advantage of an outsource team. ❞**

Working together on this major project helped the overall team, he found. 'It brought the Spanish and the Northern Europe financial communities a lot closer together than they had ever been, because of the contact we were having. We had to rely on each other. The worst thing a company can say is: "You ought to work together". You say: "Why?"'

His team uses something known as the *affinity model* to describe individual and team networks by defining exactly who does what and highlighting shared objectives and tasks. 'If you put the top 35 core activities, list the functions across the top and ask who does that activity, it shows you what functions have to do with various processes. This can be taken further, so that rather than have functional integration, you have process integration. I feel I have far more affinity with colleagues in Northern Europe than some finance people in the same office, because we have shared aims.'

'We do celebrate success. We go out for a meal. There will be a conference to reinforce the messages and bring people together; remind people we're all one team. That will be pan-European.'

Summary: advice for building successful cross-regional teams (by David Baker)

- You can't be like some consultants who come in with this wonderful new idea. You have to get the hearts and minds of the people.
- Sometimes, you find you have to adapt locally, e.g. because of the local law. This happened in France as there are restrictions on arranging rebates under accounting laws (Sapin's Law).
- People have the same motivations at work wherever they are – they want to succeed. You overcome stereotyping by getting to know people.
- Meeting and socializing away from the office can be hugely motivating.
- Including the outsource providers in the Barcelona meeting was helpful. It binds them in so they are seen as partners, not just suppliers.
- Tele-conferences are not the same as being able to look into someone's eyes, and see if they buy in to what you are saying.
- Finance teamwork with an affinity model; link people together by shared activity/responsibility. 'The worst thing a company can do is say: "You ought to work together". People say: "Why?"' Have to have shared aims.
- Celebrate success, e.g. go out for meals, publicize success.

If we don't know where we are going, we will probably end up somewhere else

The human internet does not always receive the same attention as the communications infrastructure and the business set-up and processes. The learning points at the end of this chapter provide practical ways to direct multicultural, multi-continent, multifunctional teams. Flat teams do *not* sort themselves out – they require stewardship, communication and leadership. Today's and tomorrow's directors are required to reproduce leaders in every team. They are also required to remain self-aware, adaptive and fast learners. Taking time out to think: 'How are we doing? What impact am I having on others in the team; do they trust me? Do we know in which direction we are heading? And how will we know if we have got there?' are some of the important questions we need to keep asking ourselves.

Your own human internet

Here's an exercise that can help you evaluate how you relate to the people you work with. Draw a diagram of your own personal network; including external as well as internal contacts. Describe visually the strength of those personal relationships (different people find different imagery works: a colour code; a system of lines and dotted lines; etc.). You'll notice that it is probably very different from the formal organizational drawing, but is likely to be closer to the real dynamics of the teams and networks that you belong to. It's a mini-human internet.

Put the diagram away for a few hours or days. Then take a look at it, think: this is a pictorial description of the relationships I have at work, and ask yourself: Is it a pattern that best serves the team's and my needs? Is there a weak relationship that really needs to be strengthened? Is there a broken relationship that needs mending?' Conversely, there may be a close relationship with someone who, in purely commercial terms, is not so important, or where your closeness could be cutting someone else out. This can be just as difficult to handle. It is hardly to be recommended that you start to relate less well with someone, but it might be worth considering if someone else is being neglected who may matter.

Everyone at work has these little personal networks, whether written down or not. They are very powerful, and defy structure, processes and procedures. The 20th century model of the company was based on the organizational chart, with emphasis on structure and lines of accountability. This chart may be helpful, but it does not really describe reality. The real organization is more like a brain than a structure. There are millions of neural pathways – some weak, some strong – connecting the different parts of a living and changing entity.

ᶠᶠEveryone at work has these personal networks. They are very powerful, and defy structure, processes and procedures.🍴🍴

The employee survey organization Gallup has consistently asked the question: 'Is your best friend in your workplace?' and found that a positive answer correlates strongly with better performance. The extraordinary thing, however, is that from time to time Gallup is actually criticized for including the question.

It is dubbed, according to the prejudice of our age, overly personal and 'soft', but actually its inclusion is thoroughly logical and astute. If there are plenty of strong relationships, their presence indicates an extremely powerful store of collective energy lying within. Close relationships can be a destructive dynamic, on occasion, but it is important to understand their existence rather than live in denial, assuming the formal reporting lines are all-powerful.

learning points

High performance with a globally dispersed team

1 Treat the people, the team and the corporation as being part of the same endeavour.

2 Focus and leadership are essential.

3 Integrate team-building and business planning at the same events, rather than treat them as separate exercises.

4 Not all relationships have to be close; a disinterested person is sometimes the best placed for a certain role. But trust is always essential.

5 An initial face-to-face meeting needs to: provide direction, clarify the purpose and objectives of the team; set up working procedures; define roles; begin developing trust and a sense of community; understand the pressure of local responsibilities.

6 Never waste face-to-face meetings on routine information-giving such as PowerPoint presentations. These can be sent out beforehand to facilitate debate and decision-making. Face-to-face time is rare and precious, so should be used for deepening understanding of business objectives, and for getting to know one another.

▶

7 Arrange more face-to-face meetings at the start of a change programme, new project or building a new team. This develops trust that is needed to sustain virtual relationships. A higher frequency of meetings may be necessary to recover from a crisis.

8 Hold genuinely open Q & A sessions with staff. Listen carefully to body language and for feelings, as well as words.

9 Try to vary locations for face-to-face meetings, so that they are not always at head office.

10 Remember when telephone or video conferences involve some team members who are in the same room and others are only linked by telephony; it is unequal. Include the virtual team frequently by asking appropriate questions.

11 Socializing is important, especially where teams have to co-operate closely. It shouldn't be regarded as frivolous or optional.

2

The medium and the message

key points

- There are strong pressures to limit global travel for meetings.

- Video-conferencing is currently unpopular, but it can be effective for early-stage interviewing of suppliers, and some businesses will reconsider when the technology improves.

- Establishing good relationships with colleagues does not simply relate to physical proximity; communication and trust can also exist where people work in remote locations.

- There can be over-use of meetings by single-site teams; the objective is for the right level of communication, not the maximum level.

- New media can be used to reach out to staff and to customers.

- For historical reasons, English is the universal business language. There are some useful principles of good conduct to learn for native and non-native speakers alike in business teams.

- Generation Y, those born after 1980, may have developed patterns of communicating that are distinct from older workers.

Each January, in the Swiss skiing resort of Davos, political and business leaders gather for the world's über-strategy meeting. They talk about the latest communications technology, but they still meet in person. In 2007, a combination of awareness of advances in video-technology and of the desire to curb carbon emissions, created scope for tentative discussions on the virtual conference. *The Times* of London reported:

'Davos Man and Woman have never been more conscious of their carbon footprint and so they naturally wonder aloud whether they should be travelling at all . . . tech-savvy sorts were thus discussing this strange contradiction and revealed a solution: the hologram.'

It sounds like 'Star Trek', but it could be closer than we think. Professors Todd Mowry and Seth Goldstein of Carnegie Mellon University in Pennsylvania, USA, are pioneers of the technology, and claim that it goes beyond use of mere holograms, creating replicas. Todd Mowry, who is Head of Research at semiconductor giant Intel, comments: 'The idea is to produce a physical replica that will maintain the shape and appearance of a person or object. As the person or object moves, so will the replica. The replica is a physical entity, not a hologram. You could interact with it just as if it were actually in the room with you.'

> **❝The hologram sounds like 'Star Trek', but it could be closer than we think.❞**

Todd adds: 'The motivating application for the research was to improve on today's video-conferencing. Through dynamic physical rendering, you could recreate an entire scene or environment at multiple locations. The same group of people could appear at each location, in real form or as replicas. The same furniture, whiteboards and other objects would appear at every location. Any movement or interaction with a person or object at one location would be reproduced at all of them. Every meeting could be face-to-face.'[5]

Even without green considerations, corporate budgets and the sheer pressures of time are limiting our capacity to meet face-to-face. In the case study on page 63, how the electronics giant Siemens cut its global travel budget by one third is discussed. For all these reasons, any improvement in video-conferencing technology would be seized upon with enthusiasm by business executives. There is deep dissatisfaction with current video-conference technology, with organizations citing time delays, poor image and cost, among other factors, as discussed later.

Managers need to match the medium to both the message and the wider purpose of connecting individuals. They can now select à la carte from a growing menu: face-to-face, phone conference, Messenger, blogging, and so on. Leaders need to keep asking themselves the following questions: 'Do we all have to "be there"? If so, does the meeting justify the time and cost? If not, what are we losing?'

What do we get from 'being there'?

Even if it takes place on a 'Star Trek' style holodeck, could the advanced virtual conference completely replace the face-to-face meeting? Science that shows us the benefits to communication of being in the same room. Moods are 'infectious', and most communication is through body language, eye contact and unconscious signals. In some circumstances, as little as 7 per cent of the communication is in the meaning of the words spoken, according to studies by Professor Albert Mehrabian, one of the leading researchers in the field. It is inevitable that at least some of the intensity of non-verbal communication will be lost even with advanced holograms. Terry Pearce, President of Leadership Communications and coach to senior business leaders across the globe, says: 'New neurological research tells us that when we meet face-to-face we begin to mirror the neurons of the other person or persons. Accordingly, if you listen well, you create the possibility of having the same experience as the other. That is how empathy is built. It *appears* that the closer you are physically, the better that happens.' He adds, however: 'It [closeness] is not absolutely necessary for empathy to happen – for mirror neurons to be created.'

In some circumstances, as little as 7 per cent of the communication is in the meaning of the words spoken.

The limbic part of the brain, that most associated with emotion, works 80,000 times faster than the cortex, which deals with reason. 'That's why stories work well as a means of communication,' Terry says. Does this mean that multi-site teams are doomed? The good news is that the overriding factor that creates a good team is skill in communication rather than proximity. A well crafted e-mail will engage more than a poorly handled face-to-face meeting. But for the highest levels of engagement, it is likely that meeting at least sometimes is essential. How would he approach the task of managing a dispersed team, with a limited travel budget?

'I would have a conversation with each person on the team; I would explain that the budget restrictions only allow us to meet once or twice a year; I would say: "That bothers me and here's why: it prevents me from getting to know you the way I would like to know you: your family; your values. I would like to see the place in which you operate. I would like to feel, touch and smell the environment. I would like to understand the pressures on you. If I don't know you there is no way I will be as effective leading the team as I would like to be. I'm going to make best use of the time that we do have together. My job is to make sure you know that you are supported – and accountable."

'Then, you back it up. You try to set up meetings, so that you get the personal connection. You don't waste time trying to do business before that human connection is established. You can do business on the phone. People think they should show hundreds of PowerPoint slides at a meeting to make sure that everyone has the same information. Accomplishing that task is the wrong use of this type of meeting.

'The second thing is that I might set up a remote communication system – like video-conferencing – for some meetings and then allow time for connection. Of course, you have to be sensitive to people's comfort levels, but the objective is to create trust and bring the team together. One of my clients assumed responsibility for a new [dispersed] team – most of the people were at work stations. He started each meeting focusing on one individual on the team, who had 15 minutes just to talk about themselves. They were encouraged to show pictures, even videos of the facility and their families. It was way of showing to people that they're important and building trust.'

Cynthia McCague, Senior Vice-President Human Resources at Coca-Cola, says that, though it can be used sparingly, the face-to-face meeting can be precious: 'Our team spent time together last month working on the people development forum; working on elements of change in communication for the corporation as a whole, so that other people could do that deeper work. It's very useful to have people in the room: on the flip chart you can draw pictures of what you're thinking. It's an opportunity for people to engage – or have a jolly good fight over something. I believe strongly in forming, storming, norming and performing. That happens in virtual ways; accelerated by having a team together in a focused way; not just a feel-good factor, but part of working together.'

Concetta Lanciaux, Executive Vice President Synergies at LVMH, says: 'Meeting is three-dimensional; you engage all the senses. And when people appear on a screen they are talking in a more formal way and there is less spontaneity. In our business, due to the elements of creativity and autonomy, emotional intelligence is 50 per cent of the matter. This includes the ability to make decisions; to know your way in complex situations; to adapt yourself to local businesses and cultures; the capacity to have empathy. The definition of emotional intelligence is seeing beyond the surface and reading between the lines, ability to feel empathy and to correctly interpret different situations. Video-conferencing is for people who already know each other, or who don't need to know each other. But in recruitment it can skew your impression. Finally, it is also a cultural question. In some cultures creating a personal relationship, off the record, approach is important. If I generalize, in France, a client would buy a product if he trusts the sales person, while in Germany or Japan, a client would buy if he is convinced that the product is good.'

Video-conferences: an irritation

The biggest source of irritation among executives we interviewed was the video-conference experience. Views ranged from antipathy to outright hostility. It is worth emphasizing, however, that the perception is due largely to dissatisfaction with quality, not with the concept *per se*. As standards improve on sound, picture and synchronicity, many will take another look at the medium, to see if improvements in connections can enable more fluent conversations.

❝The biggest source of irritation among executives was the video-conference experience.❞

'I hate video-conferencing,' says Sue Turner, Group HR Director of The Body Shop, part of L'Oréal. 'I don't like the time delay. Although you can see someone – maybe it's just my eyesight – but either the picture is not clear or it's just hard to pick up those nuances. It's better than not having it, but you can't have the sense of warmth of someone.'

Andy Warrender of Gore has tried 'every possible tool', but has rejected many as unnecessary or inconvenient. For meetings, the company uses either face-to-face and telephone conferencing; the latter may on occasion be supplemented by an online presentation. Video-conferencing is rarely used. 'The frustration with video-conferencing was that it fixed you to the places where you had equipment,' he says. 'The quality was dreadful. We know what each other look like anyway. Phone conferencing is so much easier. Contact is supported by a sophisticated voice-mail system allowing messages for multiple recipients, forwarding of replies, and so on.'

Alan Wigley of Intel adds: 'I would like to see improvement in video-conferencing. Most companies probably don't use it because the picture is distorted and the speech is in a different time to the picture itself. I am really surprised it isn't good. It ought to be possible to have six people on a screen. We don't use it because the technology isn't good enough, or is expensive.'

The one lone voice in favour of the medium came from Concetta Lanciaux, Executive Vice President Synergies at LVMH. She does not use video-conferences as a complete replacement for face-to-face meetings, but has found that they are valuable in whittling down a short list when interviewing potential suppliers. She is committed to travel where necessary, but will replace it where she can: 'We are dispersed. We also have a very powerful e-mail network; intranet; video-conferencing and telephone conferencing. Video-conferences are widely used to interview people – potential partners, before making a decision to go and see them. I can screen five consultants in one morning. That allows me to take into account consultants in the US, not just in France. To me, video-conferencing is one of the biggest aids in globalization. It allows you to see, when choosing an external partner. In other words, it's a way of helping you select the appropriate final option. It gets you more quickly to the result.'

It does not replace the final meeting in a selection process, Concetta reports. 'When you select, emotional intelligence is key: whether you can work with these people. All of these "soft" elements you can only judge when you are with the person in the room; but content, and whether you can present technical information; all of this can be done by video-conferencing.'

Why are we here?

You cannot see, or otherwise sense, someone's understanding of an issue completely unless you are in the same room, and there remain huge question marks over the capability of even the most advanced holographic technology to fully replicate the emotional charge. The precise manner in which someone was nodding with agreement, or the way in which their eyes lit up, on a particular shared topic of interest, can stay in the memory for years. This will strongly influence your relationship, and your appreciation of the depth of their understanding of an issue and its importance.

❝ The 'gold standard' meeting is indispensable for certain tasks. ❞

Pressure to limit the frequency of face-to-face meetings will vary from company to company, but will often be very strong. This may prevent meetings that ought better to have taken place, from a business perspective. In other situations, however, it may be a healthy discipline, forcing executives to reserve face-to-face meetings only for cases of absolute necessity. The 'gold standard' meeting – in the same room, perhaps with an opportunity to dine and socialize – is indispensable for certain tasks, summarized as:

■ In-depth strategic discussions

■ Forming a new team

■ Communication of vision and mission – giving the workforce a chance to get to know the leaders

■ For people who are going to be working closely to get to know one another

- To forge a new identity and sense of common purpose following a merger or joint venture

- Meetings may need to be more frequent than usual during a recovery phase of an organization.

But it may actually be inadvisable, rather than merely unnecessary, to have meetings for other purposes. There are opportunities that arise from global dispersal, and curious hidden advantages from limited or virtual communications. The lesson here is to be absolutely clear about the purpose of meetings; where and when they are held. It also means that we should understand in greater depth the real issues that are involved: what can and cannot be done online, and what the business risks are of ignoring these essential matters. Above all, we need to make the most of our time together.

Face-to-face can be powerful, but must be used well

Successful leaders see this issue as a leadership one, with accompanying decisions and challenges to face on communications media. They adopt an optimistic approach: transforming the human internet rather than simply dealing with a big multi-media, multi-timezone headache. They put the emphasis on getting the clearest direction, the best relationships and the strongest communicative skills, then fit the meetings arrangements to suit.

❝Trust is an absolute prerequisite.❞ Trust is an absolute prerequisite. Everyone we spoke to said this, mostly without prompting. And trust is difficult to establish without some direct meeting, with all the attendant eye contact, body language communication, and bonding. The stronger the trust established between individuals, the better able they are to communicate effectively in subsequent internet connections.

For example, Antonio Sedan, General Manager at Comai in Colombia, says that 'face-to-face meetings are still necessary to create bonds'. He goes on: 'If we have good relationships and intense virtual communications, when we meet it is like an explosion of effusiveness that creates strong bonds for future virtual communications that end in increased effectiveness. Face-to-face meetings reinforce and enhance relationships and team effectiveness.'

This development of rapport through face-to-face meetings can reduce the need for travelling over the longer term, Antonio adds. 'Travel that follows smart, well-crafted, virtual interactions are shorter. Travelling is very useful when you are able to lock in a room most of the people required to make a complex decision.' Many managers express themselves very strongly on this matter. Sue Turner, Group HR Director at The Body Shop, says: 'I still have the old-fashioned view that there's no substitute for sitting across the table or being next to someone and building a relationship of trust, understanding their experience and aspirations. I still believe fundamentally that the building block of doing business is networking, empathy and understanding. Three of the organisations I have worked with – Accenture, Barclays and L'Oréal/Body Shop – do a lot of global networking and put a high store on the camaraderie of the senior executives.'

Sue also makes the point that cultural nuances, discussed earlier, can only be well understood by visiting the region concerned. And for a close working colleague based on another continent, meeting is essential. She describes as an example her relationship with the HR Director for the US: 'When I joined we had lots of conversations on the phone, and built up a fine relationship. It wasn't until I went out there and spent a week talking and working around her territory that I really had empathy for the issues that she is facing. Unless you have empathy you cannot relate – you're using a different language. That's when the body language helps. The L'Oréal Integration Director, whom I spend a lot of time talking to, has very good English, but we might be prone to misunderstanding each other if we didn't spend a lot of time face-to-face. If I am in a meeting with him, asking searching questions on L'Oréal policy, he may shrug his shoulders, which is a very French gesture, or just smile. What that says is, "C'est la vie" or "I can't take this any further". If you try to communicate that in words it's very difficult. Even a raised eyebrow can convey a message. If you are trying to work out what's possible from a negotiation, closed or open body language gives you a clue.'

All businesses are people businesses

Leslie Van de Walle, President Shell Retail (now CEO at Rexam), says: 'I have a strong view on this. You cannot run a business from head office and not meet face-to-face. I know it's not flavour of the month. I spend 60 per cent of my time travelling. My business is a people business – you cannot relate through technology; you use it very carefully. One of the reasons the business is successful is the amount of time spent together. I haven't found a better way than face-to-face [though] it depends on your type of business. Some people don't like personal contact; they shouldn't travel a lot and do lots of face-to-face meetings.'

'What I get – I don't have the metrics – but in Shell those units meeting most are by far the most motivated and best run. The feedback we get from people is that meetings are also very motivated, helpful and always insightful. I'm sure for me that it works.'

Allon Bloch, a venture capitalist based in Israel, also says: 'Trust is difficult to build, but once you build it you can do lots of things, and you don't need face-to-face meetings [so much]. I go to the States every six to eight weeks and I'm presenting to my CEOs every two to three months. With a number of them I make many phone calls.'

At Gore-Tex and medical products manufacturer Gore, the organizational values of high engagement and communication that it has sought to maintain as it has become global, mean that air travel bills are considerable. Andy Warrender, leader of the fabrics division, does report that some observers have commented: 'You must be crazy: it's inefficient to have all that travel.' But he concludes: 'The flipside is the return on investment we get from people; the engagement, the passion, the commitment, the belief. One of the things we do is an annual employee survey. Over the years, on the question, "I like working at Gore" on a score of 0 to 9, we have scored consistently over 8 (with 9 being, "I completely agree with this statement").'

In passing, it is valid to question the logic of referring to the pursuit of employee engagement as a 'crazy' endeavour. This example of Gore, which has an unbroken record of commercial success and expansion over half a century, bears out once again the finding of the Hawthorne experiments three-quarters of a century ago: that the engagement and motivation of a company's people is the single most important determinant of success. Accepted by most both in theory and in practice, it remains puzzlingly the exception, not the norm. It rarely features as a strategic priority, despite greater consistency in yielding returns compared with, for example, merger activity.

The principle holds for virtual communication, too. Andy Warrender at Gore has always had a policy of replying to a message within 24 hours. The principle is inculcated into his team, and people will challenge each other if it is not upheld. This greatly assists the effectiveness of any messaging system. 'When we began to form an international element the founder Bill Gore wanted to copy this direct one-to-one communication,' says Andy Warrender.

A level playing field in the same room

Face-to-face meetings can be more democratic than tele- or video-conferences. For example, a group at the head office enjoying the benefit of being in the same room together, while country representatives join in the meeting via a video-link or telephone link, can dominate discussion. This will especially be the case if they are native speakers in the principal language of the company. Global chip-manufacturer Intel, in its compensation and expenses team for the EMEA (Europe, Middle East and Africa) region, has replaced some telephone conferencing with face-to-face meetings for this reason. Alan Wigley is Payments Manager for the region, with 29 team members stretched across ten countries. He says: 'The first thing I wanted to do [after joining] was travel and meet everyone. I joined from Pizza Express, which was purely UK and Ireland. I feel that anyone new has to create a new team. When I joined I made sure the quarterly meetings were face-to-face. Previously they were on the phone. I felt that that didn't work, especially when dominated by a large number of people from one country in one room. If, from the UK, there were four or five people in attendance, and from other countries just one person, this person was more of an observer than a participant. So the individual from Russia was just a listener, not a contributor. You have to have a strong personality to overcome that. Getting input from everyone can bring out more contributions from people. When they are present, they are involved straight away.'

Alan adds: 'I think that, regardless of whether people are overseas or local, knowing someone face-to-face and meeting them brings that trust. We always trust someone more whom we've met – that you feel that if they say they will do something for you, you feel they will. It makes people more accountable. I don't know why, but it does.'

David Grigson, CFO of media giant Reuters, has similar experiences: 'My biggest frustration with technology is that it doesn't always do what it's intended to do. Connections are lost or there is too much noise interference. We've all been on tele-conferences from far-away places where it's hard to make the connection and even harder to stay connected for the full length of the meeting. With the majority of the team in a room, and the remainder dialling in, it is always hard for those dialling in to feel part of the meeting. They are not part of the banter that goes on when people are settling down or during the breaks.'

David is a member of four teams: the main board, a small group executive committee that meets weekly, a larger leadership team that meets every two months, and the finance team, which he heads. He devotes considerable attention to his own team, consisting of six senior finance leaders. 'As well as meetings I hold performance review meetings with every one of my direct reports monthly. These monthly Performance Review Meetings are intended to be able to give, and receive, regular feedback on performance against objectives. We also find time to talk at a more personal level – what's going on in their lives, things like pressures, priorities, work-life balance. I keep in touch with them as individuals, whether they are around the office here, or overseas, so that when we do see each other there is no sense that I have lost touch with them simply because they are not working in the same location as me. We also hold weekly [tele-conference] meetings. These take place at lunch-time in the UK when it's breakfast time in New York and early evening in Singapore. It's limited to an hour and we stick rigidly to the schedule time.'

Ian Adamson of SSL says: 'E-mails encourage more frequent dialogue and communication – not necessarily all good – but for me they represent no way to build a team; no way to build a vision and shared goals and objectives. It's convenient. It works because, for example, you can sit in an airline lounge and send e-mails and maximize time – but as the primary communication tool, it is not my favourite option. Give me a one-on-one meeting any day. Neither am I a big fan of video-conferences. I think to some extent it shows a lack of commitment – that you couldn't be bothered to make the journey to be there in person. However, there are times when video-conferencing is essential. For example we have factories in China and India and it is important to meet the people there too.'

❝ Give me one-on-one any day . . . ❞

An international team *can* really fire

It is by no means always the case that a dilution or a trade-off in team engagement is involved when working internationally. There are many factors at play: how the team was selected; whether they get a 'buzz' from international working; how they feel about each other; the sense of purpose; how comfortable they are with virtual communications. The architecture of a well-crafted series of face-to-face meetings can create a foundation for strong online relationships. However, it pays to remember that domineering, aggressive managers can very quickly 'suck the oxygen out of the room', leaving team members and staff de-energized and turned off. Leadership style is as important as what and how managers communicate.

It is possible to achieve high levels of cohesion and achievement in a multi-site team. Conor Gallagher, Project Manager at software giant

SAP, for example, recalls one experience as part of a pioneering team of software specialists: 'In terms of pay and rations people reported to their home country, but as a team we had the same manager. We worked the same projects together. We rarely met; just once a year we had a get-together. We had a strong *esprit de corps* but didn't meet very often. At the time we had a strong sense of identity. We were the best consultants in the market, we were led to believe. The work was important; we were jetting off to places at short notice.'

In a similar vein Concetta Lanciaux, Executive Vice-President Synergies of LVMH, comments: 'Contact with people does not equal geographic proximity. It's not mathematical. It's related to the necessity to see the person; the pleasure of talking to the person and what you learn from that person. These three – necessity, pleasure and learning – determine the number of contacts. You can see the people who work together and the people who don't. Often people say: "I don't like to work with them". I always try to create teams that are compatible which means that I don't put people together who are the same. Concerning the distance, I admit that I am much closer to some people in New York than to some people next door. Liking to work with each other is an important element of business success. As a matter of fact enjoying working with your colleagues is one of the most powerful motivation factors a company can provide to an employee. Some 80 per cent of the time you recruit someone on skills, but 80 per cent when someone is fired it is because he did not fit in. This is one of the most important parameters when recruiting someone: will he fit into the team from a cultural perspective? This is why strong company values and culture is so important.'

Benefits to being the virtual stranger

Dispersal can be a problem. But sometimes, proximity is an issue! It is often commented on that office workers see more of their colleagues than of their partners and friends, and that this can be a difficulty. Working in the flat world can lessen this, with more home working, for example, and the motivational plus can outweigh the practical difficulties of dispersal. We all get under each other's feet from time to time, and can value the

Are there hidden advantages to the virtual connection?

There some advantages of e-mail and Messenger over face-to-face meetings. For example, it is common nowadays for meetings not to be minuted. With e-mail and Messenger, you have an accurate historical record of what was said – which can help business planning; and help avoid misunderstandings and miscommunications. Hindsight is not always 20:20. People often have different memories of events and meetings. There is a tendency – stronger in some people than in others – to use events to create a story or a version, rather than recall accurately. The case study above of Flores de America showed how the managers there use transcripts from Messenger to save directly to archive.

❝ The trick is to use different media for what they are best suited. ❞

The trick is to use different media for what they are best suited. Messenger can be extremely useful for an intellectual exchange of ideas, for example. We now have more choice of media. With greater choice we have more communicative resources, enabling us to tailor the right medium for the right purpose. What matters is not necessarily *more* communication; but better communication.

Those who are most adept at operating in the flat world see the multitude of ways of connecting with people as a rich and exciting complement to more traditional forms of communicating and meeting. Teoh Swee Lin, a consultant at Sheppard Moscow, worked until recently as the head of a regional consulting team for a major software company. She was based in Singapore, with three direct reports – one in Singapore, one in India, one in Australia. Another team member had a 'dotted line' relationship to her from Hong Kong. The team's area of coverage was 13 countries in the Asia-Pacific region. 'In that set-up, the team provided services to our end-customers across these countries through country teams,' she says.

Swee Lin further states: 'There are instances when I see it [virtual communication] as a problem – this is when we rely only on the virtual communications, for example using e-mail to negotiate or argue a point and thinking that it's good enough. That's when a point may get misinterpreted. But if we use e-mail to communicate the information before a negotiation or a debate, it allows both parties to be better prepared.

'In my mind virtual communications allow us to be more effective in what we do, because we are now able to do a lot more than we used to – for example, communicate with people whom we'd otherwise not have the opportunity to cross paths with at all; communicate with people a lot more frequently than we'd otherwise be able to, have more avenues for communication.'

Swee Lin adds: 'I used to do weekly operations calls via teleconference with my direct reports, and monthly calls with my peers from the other regions – EMEA, North America and South America. The monthly calls included the global consulting lead facilitator, we used that meeting to countercheck our strategies, budgets and execution process. If we didn't have virtual communications to allow this to happen, I would have had to clock up more travel time and expenses or else have much less communication then is necessary to successfully run the practice.'

Swee Lin even recruited people whom she had not met in person – but note that she relied heavily upon relationships of trust with people who had met them. 'I actually recruited two people in Australia without having met them face-to-face; by relying on a mixture of my internal networks there – making sure they knew what I would look for if I was interviewing them face-to-face. They proved to be very reliable recruits – and of course I had the first and last interview with each over the phone. Both interviews lasted at least an hour. I also recruited the person in India over the phone too. In this case, I also used teleconference facilities because I wanted to get a sense of how he looked and behaved before I recruited him. I was more rigorous in this case because I wasn't as sure after the first telephone interview and wanted additional data points to help me arrive at a decision.'

On what basis did she feel so confident to recruit without meeting? 'I had been involved in quite a bit of recruitment before. It was taking my intuition and judgement about people to the phone. If it had been my first few recruits, I wouldn't have been as confident. I guess the other thing was trusting the judgement of people whom I delegated the face-to-face interviews to. If I already felt comfortable with a person over the phone, I'd feed back to the people [colleagues] what I wanted verification on, so that they could give me a firsthand view of it. I would only request those whose judgement I trusted to be involved in the interviews; plus ensure that they also had a stake in the success of the interviews. Once the candidates were recruited, I made sure that their orientation was face-to-face – they were brought on site and we spent time working with one another before they went back to their home base.'

What is interesting about Swee Lin's experience is that it is probably *more* thorough than some conventional recruiting processes: there is more than one person's judgement taken into account; a series of interview loops; and all interviewers hold a stake in the success of the hire. In all global transactions or decisions, we need to be clear about the robustness of the process and the relationships first, before deciding on the specific media for each task. Put another way: make sure the human internet is set up correctly before deciding on which parts of the electronic one are going to assist you for which details of the process.

❝If a dispersed team is not communicating well, it may not be because of the dispersal.❞

If a dispersed team is not communicating well, it may not be because of the dispersal – just as a multinational team may not be struggling because of culture. Some team members are not on speaking terms with one another even though they are all in the same open-plan office. Their communication, and possibly their relationships, might actually be improved if they were on opposite sides of the world.

Native or non-native English? Some notes on language

English is to business language what Microsoft is to software. It is not necessarily the best, but it has become the one that everyone uses, with the attendant benefit that everyone only has to learn one, in addition to the native tongue. This is unlikely to change over the course of the next century.

Where everyone in a business team has English as a second language, there is a clear equality, with 'everyone at an equal disadvantage'. Many international teams feature some members who are native English speakers, and others who are not. For this common situation, there are certain principles of good conduct to observe, especially for native speakers. These are:

- Avoid jargon and other metaphors. This is a good principle in any case, but is essential when dealing with people for whom English is a second language. Terms like 'leverage' are metaphorical and imprecise. Try instead to use active verbs, and to specify who will be doing what. So instead of saying: 'We want you to leverage the benefits of the new acquisition', say: 'We want you to meet regularly with the executives of the new acquisition and produce a joint plan on products and services.'

- Speak clearly, especially if you have a strong regional accent. People won't feel patronized if you slow down a little. If there's a choice between a formal word and a colloquialism, choose the formal word.

- If a non-native speaker has a heavy accent, be patient and listen carefully (this is usually easier in face-to-face meetings where gestures can be reassuring and helpful). Imagine how well you would fare speaking their language.

- A native English speaker can generate goodwill by speaking in another tongue, where the occasion suits. Ian Adamson, European Managing Director of SSL, says: 'The Italian team were holding their annual conference and I was invited to join them for the event. I was asked to present to them, so I learned the speech in Italian – a language which I don't speak – and I'm pleased to say it went down really well. That's what I mean by respect. It's probably the most frightening thing I've ever done.'

- If you are not a native English speaker, and an English speaker addresses you in your tongue, reply in this language. This is respectful and acknowledges the effort they have made. You can later revert to English if that is the more effective for communication.

■ For certain negotiations, especially where legal terminology is involved and the stakes are high, it is advisable to employ professional interpreters.

Onward with travel

It is difficult to be certain whether technological advances and pressures to curb travel will have a serious impact on the frequency of physical meetings of international teams. It is probably too soon to switch out of airline stocks. When world leaders replace their annual get-together in Davos with a giant holographic conference – that would be the sign that things have changed.

learning points

How to get the meeting structure right

1 Remember that communication is not just about sharing facts and downloading information. Inspiring and aligning to values, mission and vision are key in the role of any leader.

2 Treat communication as a skill and as a priority that must be maintained irrespective of geographical location, frequency of face-to-face meetings and available media.

3 Match the meeting to the need: face-to-face meetings should be reserved for when they are essential.

4 Make sure the human internet is set up correctly before deciding on which parts of the electronic one are the best media for your organization.

5 Quick and frequent conversations between team members seem to be the very effective. Use texting, Messenger, etc. if the team is dispersed.

6 There are certain advantages to remote working: an absence of meeting overload, and better use of less frequent meetings. Messenger is valuable for creating a permanent record of discussions.

▶

> **❝Inspiring and aligning to values, mission and vision are key in the role of any leader.❞**

7 If a dispersed team is not communicating well, it may not actually be because of the dispersal – just as a multinational team may not be struggling because of culture. Look at the team selection and dynamics, rather than just blaming communications infrastructure or 'culture'. Your impact on others may need to be reviewed.

8 Insist on meeting from time to time.

9 Coach native English speakers on clarity of speech and sensitivity to others.

10 Have formal meetings and, where individuals are in the same office, encourage corridor conversations.

11 Communicate often, but reserve meetings for where there is a real need.

12 When you do get together don't waste time on PowerPoint presentations.

13 Remember that communication is about facts *and* feelings, not just facts. Find out not only what people think about the business plan, strategy or structure, but also how they feel about it.

14 When not meeting face-to-face, remember that non-verbal communications are lost – you may need to make additional verbal requests to ensure that people have understood and are agreed on content and action.

3

Does culture still matter?

key points

- An increasing number of individuals have dual or multi-nationality, and culturally mixed families are now commonplace.
- Cultural differences based on nation and region are still influential, but different personality types can be found in all regions.
- There can be 'cultural' differences based on age or organization, and differences of particular relevance in business teams are differences based on profession.
- Some human needs – for advancement, recognition, affiliation and opportunity – are universal.

Theories of national characteristics have been dominant as a tool in the management of multinational teams in recent years. Their use has reached a peak just as the very concept of the national character has arguably begun a long-term decline. Cheap air travel and mass migration have meant that many people are no longer living in the land of their birth, and many are of dual nationality.

Many interviewees were of a different nationality from the nominal home country of their employer; for example Miles Flint at Sony Ericsson is British, Leslie Van de Walle at Rexam is French as is Concetta Lanciaux at LVMH, and so on. North Americans and Europeans are moving to Asia to experience the faster pace of growth and opportunities it provides – something almost unheard of ten years ago, unless it was accompanied by a generous expatriate package and wonderful lifestyle.

One interviewee, Emmanuelle Chambon, is French, and grew up in France, but has lived nearly all of her adult life in India, where she set up and ran an import business, and in the UK. Her partner is half-Indian, half-English. She has two children, one born in India, one in England. She works for the France-based steel company Arcelor, recently taken over by India-based Mittal, on the Honda account in the UK. 'When I'm in the UK I see myself as being French, but when in France I see myself as being not so French. The differences, I would say, are that when I'm in the UK and I feel French, I am maybe a bit more up-front than the English. The English are still more polite and reserved. I didn't grow up here. In terms of reading interests, and food, I am French [but] when I go to France I find that people are very up-front; sometimes a little in an unsettled manner – more choleric.'

Maria-Rey Marston, Executive Director of the Latin America Logistics Center and a Colombian national, makes the point most forcefully that shared experience and interest count for far more than national-ity in terms of shared values: 'If I go to Bogotá and meet someone I was at high school with, I have nothing in common with that person. She doesn't have a PDA (Personal Digital Assistant), has not worked abroad, doesn't have Skype. My best friend is from Calcutta, but grew up in Canada, went to the Massuchusetts Institute of Technology where she met her husband, who is German, and she lives in Dusseldorf. She's absolutely my best friend. I have nothing in common with that background or language. Our commonality is experiences we've been exposed to over the past ten years.'

ᶠᶠDifferent is not wrong. ᴶᴶ The likely explanation is that the impact of culture is still quite pronounced, but that it cuts across national borders, and finds its place alongside other common points of reference. One of the positive contributions of work on cultural background by such thinkers as Fons Trompenaars is to encourage the attitude that 'different is not wrong'.

One Indian national who is head of global sourcing at a major corpo-ration in India, says that norms of negotiation are one area where national characteristics come to the fore: 'Dealing with Japanese people requires a softness, deference, lack of conflict or argument and patience. The Americans, on the other hand, walk all over you if you are not clear, articulate and ready for debate and action. Each time I am on the phone to different people all over the world I need to consciously adapt my style.'

Concetta Lanciaux, Executive Vice-President Synergies at luxury branded goods group LVMH, observes contrasting traits between the US and Japan when it comes to appraising direct reports: 'When you receive the results, in the US everyone is "outstanding"; in Japan, no one is. You have to interpret the results! Cultural differences must be respected, but cultural differences do not prevent you from adopting global policies. It's the application of the policy that changes. We have to have performance appraisals, but we have to know that in Japan there will usually be two graded "outstanding" and in the US, fifteen. They are valid in both cases.'

One of the biggest cultural differences in business concerns attitudes towards dining and hospitality, according to Sue Turner, Group HR Director at UK-based The Body Shop, owned by France-based L'Oréal. She says: 'At L'Oréal there is an executive dining room rather than staff canteen and you have a three-course lunch with wine. You are greeted at the door by a *maître d'*. I imagine that's how Barclays was in the 1950s. I went to Clichy [home to the L'Oréal headquarters] as a relatively important visitor; I was taken to the dining room. Normally I just like to eat a salad at lunchtime at most. But I thought that to have one course and no wine could be seen as being offensive. It's the same in Taiwan, where I had lunch with the head franchisee. We were taken to the best restaurant in Taipei and afforded a real feast. There was no selection; and we were expected to participate in every course. The sense of hospitality is completely different – there's no sense in requesting eating preferences as you would in an Anglo-Saxon country. So perhaps France and some Asian countries are close to each other, from the perspective of hospitality.'

The media giant Reuters operates in just about every country there is, and has made some progress in promoting diversity at management levels. Reuters' Chief Finance Officer David Grigson says that there are natural strengths from being more diverse, drawing upon 'a different set of understandings or insights', and that this can only be done by acknowledging that people may have different ways of expressing themselves. 'What we have done is make sure that our management teams are as diverse as they can be and we really see the benefits during meetings. For example the Singaporean on my management team is very measured and rarely willing to speak up unless he is absolutely sure of himself. So when he does step forward, we're all very attentive and confident in his contribution. The Brits around the table are generally more inclined to shoot from the hip.'

But cultural differences explain only a part of our way of operating, and that it is essential to get to know the unique personality underneath. Antonio Sedan of Comai in Colombia comments: 'It has not worked to try to behave according to what you learn in a course on how to deal with different cultures, because within each culture there are 1,000 reasons why people think and behave differently.'

❝Within each culture there are 1,000 reasons why people think and behave differently.❞

Miles Flint, Global President Sony Ericsson Europe, takes a similar view. 'I have always taken the view that the differences between individuals are much more personality-based, and much less nationality-based. Years ago, I was in a group of individuals, where about a quarter were Japanese, and we all did [psychometric test] Myers Briggs. There were as many personality differences within the Japanese group as among the group as a whole. You have this perception of a more unified culture than there is. People are people. A lot of cultural aspects are signposts and conventions that are an overlay. Universally, everyone is subject to Maslow's needs: firstly to clothe and feed ourselves; also people want to be in businesses that are successful; they want to succeed, individually and collectively. That's a common bond and a value across cultures that is more important than the cultural differences. I would say that that is my starting point. Subsequently, the work we did with Fons Trompenaars did identify that there are important cultural differences that need to be understood, not least within Europe. That's just as important, but one sits on top of the other. It's no good trying to explain it just with cultural differences.'

National culture is only one factor to take into account, and should never be understood in a superficial way, giving rise to stereotypes or caricatures. It is still common to hear comments such as: 'So and so is typically Japanese/Indian/German' and so on. This is a real barrier to building trust in teams and with external relationships. Another subtle barrier can be the topic of social conversation, or the form of socializing. Are you are a mostly male group talking endlessly about the cricket, or the baseball? Have you considered that someone who doesn't share your interests is being excluded from a part of team-building conversation – socializing – that is absolutely essential?

Leslie Van de Walle, President Shell Retail (appointed as CEO of Rexam since interview), comments: 'Yes, there are national differences: Latino people are much more emotional, touchy-feely. Anglo-Saxons are more reserved and intellectually driven, especially at Shell. Austrians are more organized and Asian people are quiet; often in listening mode, and self-restrained. The way I deal with it is to be sensitive about it. There are also differences between genders. We try to have diversity, understanding and awareness. I encourage people to be open about what they like to do and don't like to do. We do a lot of coaching. People say: "I didn't feel good about that decision". I try to create a climate where people are comfortable about being different, and are able to share differences. My role is to play a strong role; be coach. I may say to Asian people: "Life is unfair; you have to shout to be heard". Shell does a lot on diversity and inclusiveness, so we get a lot of coaching for the team. That's because it gives immediate feedback.'

Is there a Generation Y?

Those aged under 30 have grown up with the internet; they may have been the first in their family to visit a website, use e-mail, write a blog. Can we say that they are quite comfortable with virtual connections, and have less of a need for face-to-face meetings? This would be a dangerous assumption – after all, as we have seen above, much use of internet connections is a precursor to meeting in person. But it is worthy of some reflection.

With all the health warnings that need to be issued when attributing certain characteristics to a generation – along with culture, gender and so on, it is worth noting that there are shifts in attitudes as generations change. One only has to consider the baby boomers now retiring to note that they are not adopting the same habits or interests as their parents did. They don't want pipes, slippers and cardigans in retirement. It is at least possible that the generation growing up with the internet is going to be similarly distinct from their parents in ways that are only beginning to be discerned. The so-called 'Generation Y' (definitions vary, but typically it refers to those born since 1980) exert particular fascination in the US, as they represent a second baby boom and are more numerous than Generation X (1965–1980).

Characteristics of Generation Y appear to be, in addition to being tech-savvy: a low threshold for boredom, a disinclination to look for the 'job for life' and a strong desire to work collaboratively. This makes them ideally suited, it would seem, for working in flat global teams. That does not mean that there will not be challenges, however. If baby boomers have a tendency to over-rely on the traditional meeting, it could be that Generation Y team members may shy away from it, preferring to connect over the computer at the same time as the i-Pod constantly pipes in music. When dealing with a Generation Y colleague, they aren't going to say: 'What's that?' when you suggest a conversation via Messenger or blogging, but chairing a meeting around a desk might be a novel experience.

A feature in *USA Today* noted: 'For most students, checking messages – text, e-mail, phone, IM or messages left on social networking sites – is an almost constant pastime. "The first thing you do in the morning is check your e-mail and see if your classes are cancelled," says Amy Whidiger, 22, a senior political science major.' But the article adds: 'This shift in communication from the more personal to the digital worries some, including John Gardner of the Policy Center on the First Year of College, a non-profit education think tank. "The communication revolution has certainly improved the frequency of communication, but I'm not persuaded it has improved the quality of it at all," he says. "It certainly does not lend itself to in-depth, face-to-face conversation. If you can e-mail, voice-mail or text-message folks several times a day, you may be less likely to have dinner with them."

'Young people say their devices help them socialize. Student Nick Caine says that some bring laptops to parties "because if there's no music around, it becomes a portable stereo." Chris Allen, 22, a Ball State senior majoring in religious studies, says text messaging and using cell phones are a big help in getting together. "If you do happen upon something fun and cool that's going on, you try to find people to join in, or you call people to avoid it – don't come here."'[6]

The ultimate health warning to issue is the reminder that some core human needs – for affiliation, recognition, respect – are universal to all people of all backgrounds and ages. Awareness of generational preferences for means of communication is worth possessing, but there will be many variations within each generational category that the marketing profession defines.

Is it really culture?

Many national differences are not really cultural at all, but reflect economic and political history. Inevitably, a high proportion of people in the rapidly developing regions of the world are demonstrably ambitious. One manager made this observation of China in particular. 'They want to achieve in five years what they were denied in the past 50.'

Several times, when asked about China, our interviewees simply said: 'Huge work ethic.' That's not a cultural trait. Similarly, in western Europe, tens of thousands of people from Poland are flooding in to take up the many job vacancies. They too demonstrate a strong work ethic. But in many cases there are a similar number of unemployed people in the richer countries who remain on state welfare payments who are not prepared to take on some of the more lowly positions in hospitality, retail, agriculture or food processing. The migrant workers are only too happy to accept these positions in order to gain experience and start earning hard currency to send home or build a better life.

While businesses restructure rapidly, the practical challenges within an international team remain. These include: How do you inspire each other? How do you communicate? How do you meet deadlines? How do you resolve disputes? You may relish the idea of working in a different country, but be unprepared for the very different approaches to deadlines, teamwork, role of the boss, and other matters heavily influenced by culture.

Key to unlocking these doors is understanding the apparent paradox that 'we are all different; yet we are all the same'. Cultural differences only explain so much. We are all made from the same human putty, with the same range of expectations and personality types. So it is useful to distinguish matters where culture has a major bearing; and those where universal humanistic principles apply.

In which ways do we differ?

At the risk both of generalizing and missing certain aspects, and concentrating on matters that affect approaches to work, one could break down the matters that are primarily culturally driven as:

- Formality of address, and acceptability of sharing personal information
- Formality versus flexibility of meeting structure
- Degree to which the team discusses issues, and degree to which one is expected to proceed on one's own, i.e. is the culture extroverted or introverted?
- Sense of urgency and importance of deadlines
- Hierarchy and respect towards the boss
- Sense of responsibility versus sense of commercial freedom for the senior executives.

Experience informs us that norms in different regions do differ. For those who have lived mostly in the country of their birth, exposure to a new culture can be a shock, and half-a-dozen minor differences over matters such as punctuality, formality, manner of addressing the boss, and so on, can combine to create a disorientating experience. Without awareness of cultural traits, it is harder to identify the common human needs that lie underneath – which may seem something of a paradox.

The likely explanation is that cultural differences describe tendencies, not rules. It is probably more accurate to conceive of a 'bell curve' distribution in each population of key traits. The bell curves are different, but they overlap. For example, one interviewee described a conflict that arose in a team where a German line manager asked a Greek colleague to propose a deadline for the project on which he was working. He suggested a date some four weeks away, which was agreed to, and heard nothing more. The project was delivered one day late. The manager was angry about this; for him a deadline was a deadline. His Greek colleague in turn was angry, saying that he should have known that it was an extremely demanding deadline, and that the manager had never bothered to call and find out how it was going in the course of the project. The fact that the two formed parts of an international team made resolution of the difference difficult.

An assumption on one side of formality and introversion ('*a deadline is a deadline and just get on with it*') clashed with an expectation of informality and extroversion ('*a demanding deadline may require flexibility, and continual communication is always essential*'). However, another manager described a very similar clash of style, and consequent misunderstanding, between two individuals who were both British, working in the same office.

In which ways are we 'all the same'?

The aspects where we are 'all the same' tend to concern the following expectations we have of the psychological contract at work:

■ Being treated with respect; while a lack of knowledge of a culture can give rise to the accidental *faux pas* that can imply lack of respect, a sensitive and culturally aware person will be concerned with this, and will ask for checks and reassurance.

- Being consulted and involved.

- Having a sense of a future at the organization, with prospects.

- Having a sense of belonging and co-ownership of a team, project or corporation.

In business situations, groups communicate and work together if the bulk of the members want to, rather than whether they can, should or are theoretically incentivized to do so. Communication with people from diverse cultures and languages requires an emotional commit-

❝Communication requires an emotional commitment to engage.❞

ment to engage, and a desire to learn. Such individuals see cultural variances as points of difference, but not as barriers to mutual understanding – more an indication of different routes to the same goal.

Anyone who has learned a foreign language will have discovered that the intellectual discipline is only part of the challenge. There is a heavy dependence, especially early in the process, upon the patience and emotional intelligence of the individual with whom you are conversing – as well as your own, of course. You can have quite a successful exchange of information based upon limited vocabulary, with someone who is determined to understand you. By contrast you can have a frustrating time even at an advanced stage if your interlocutor is trying to trip you up. One can have productive working relationships that span cultures and the globe; and of course one can have seriously dysfunctional situations in teams that work in the same office, comprising just one social or ethnic group. But the effort and personal development required to work in a diverse, widely-dispersed group, is likely to be greater.

Monika Altmaier, Project Leader Internationalization, Siemens Business Services

Monika Altmaier has been involved in virtual teaming for more than seven years. Her team consists of ten people located in Germany, Italy, Belgium, the UK, Austria, Greece, Australia, the USA and Singapore. They meet around twice a year, relying for the rest of the time on conference calls, online conversations via Messenger and video-conferencing using Siemens' own Centra technology. Siemens has sharply cut back its once huge annual travel budget – by around one third. She says that reduced travel expenses, and better use of time, can minimize the cost of arranging and supporting face-to-face meetings, but fully acknowledges that this is a major shift requiring investment in personal and group skills to make it work.

Monika's approach to virtual teams is to communicate often and continuously, dispel fear, build-up confidence and create new perspectives through involvement, motivation and reward. She finds that, while technological advances have been of huge benefit in assisting communication and understanding within teams, it is still essential that they meet from time to time. An important principle, she finds, is that there are face-to-face meetings and team-building exercises at the formation of a team.

❝It is easier to overcome the limitations of virtual contact if there is a rapport between individuals.❞

This builds up a bank of goodwill and trust that one relies upon for communicating with and understanding each other in the course of the team's work. It is much easier to overcome the limitations of virtual contact if there is a rapport and bond of trust between individuals.

Monika's experience is that there is universality of human need on essential aspects such as respect, dignity and opportunity for advancement. 'What we have in common is that we do want to be treated with respect. You also need to appreciate and value differences. Honest and timely feedback is important, so that people are rewarded and treated with dignity; also, having opportunities to learn and to unlock their full potential, have fun and enjoy what they are doing and feel passionate about it.'

The line manager has to be able to manage him/herself, and needs to work even harder than in a geographically close team to give clear direction and communicate individual expectations to each member, so

▶

that they know what is expected of them. A written definition of an individual's role and objectives helps.

Negative feedback needs particularly sensitive handling when you cannot meet the person face-to-face. What to do when there is a weekly scheduled conference call and one person frequently doesn't attend, saying they 'forgot'? This used to happen in a company that Monika previously worked for. She says: 'The ways in which feedback is given varies widely across cultures. The approaches I use include: separating feedback from the person; mixing negative with positive; using "I" statements wherever possible, providing specific feedback one-to-one. Another is not letting others lose face – this is especially important in Asian countries, which is why an indirect feedback is often necessary.'

Some surprising events can occur, that may depend upon differing attitudes to hierarchy, she has found. For example, it may be decided that a product launch is on the 14th of the month. Then France says

❝Everything is a negotiation.❞

that this is not convenient because it is a public holiday; Italy says that it is not a good day for their team, and the line manager's ambition for a single, focused launch day for PR activity begins to unravel. This highlights how the modern corporation often is not a hierarchical, colonial structure any more, and that 'everything is a negotiation', in the words of one manager.

'We work virtually, across time zones; we have two sessions – early morning in German time, so that people in Singapore and Australia can participate; and in the afternoon, so that people in the US can take part. We had a conference call – I was leader of this group – and one person did not take part. I asked him and he said he "simply forgot". There is much more co-ordination time for the one leading the team if you have to send e-mail reminders.'

One area where she finds that there is a cultural difference is in assumptions around the structure and purpose of meetings. In Germany, there is an expectation of a tightly structured meeting, focused closely on agenda items. Participants are expected to consider each matter carefully and prepare beforehand, so that the meeting is a final stage in a process, where people meet to reach a decision. 'By contrast, Americans will engage more in "brainstorming" issues and in open discussions. 'They say: "What's the point of meeting when you know from the beginning what the outcome should be?",' says Monika. 'The Americans do much more actually in the meeting, and not before.'

Neither approach is necessarily right or wrong; it may depend upon the purpose of the meeting – or it may be appropriate to seek a balance between the approaches. If there is too much preplanning and structure, people can feel uninvolved in the procedure, and important ideas may get missed. But engage too much in brainstorming, and the group can waste time on unimportant matters, and lose sight of the sense of commercial priority that a carefully designed agenda ought to bring to the process. As Monika notes: 'I prefer a mixture of the German and American approaches to meetings. At the beginning of team formation, when you are not used to working together, you need a team-building phase; the more you can do as a group, the more openly you can communicate, the better. But sometimes you do need to be more direct.'

One other area where cultural differences come into play is in directness of language. In Germany and the Netherlands, it is possible to be quite directly critical of someone else, without incurring serious repercussions. This is less possible in Asian cultures, where to lose face openly can be devastating. 'No one likes it but in Germany you can do it,' Monika observes. She has learned to give feedback in the form: 'I feel like this when you do that,' which honestly expresses her perspective, without ducking the responsibility of giving feedback on an individual's performance.

❝Diversity of background creates the potential for more creativity.❞

Diversity of background represents a strength that Monika seeks to harness. It creates the potential for there to be more creativity; different ways of solving problems or creating new services.

Monika Altmaier's top five tips for virtual teams are:

- Define a virtual team's goals at the outset.
- Let inexperienced people work with experienced people.
- Build trust remotely through communication and communities.
- Embark upon virtual teams as a company-wide project hand-in-hand with change management initiatives.
- Standardize the virtual teaming process across the company.

European top team

A European board from a telecommunications agency SO had been specifically recruited to turn around a stagnating business with huge potential. This was achieved by hiring top talent from a variety of regions including Spain, Italy, Germany, UK, France, Holland, Sweden and Poland.

All these country managers had, within a six-month period under the guidance of their CEO, come to grips with the issues and markets in their own countries. The trend was starting to change, but they lacked an overall pan-European strategy, which could only be achieved by beginning to work together. The whole now needed to become more than simply the sum of the parts. What was clear at the outset was that they all had a great deal of respect for each other's functional and technical capability as business leaders in their own right. They did, however, get 'stuck' in thinking how they might work together. This was being imposed by pan-European customers, such as Carrefour and L'Oréal, and the demands of a cross-regional supply chain, installation of SAP software and career development opportunities for themselves and their teams.

Most of the team had built up cultural stereotypes of other countries. This allowed them to find excuses of 'why it was *not* possible to work together'. If the English were always simply distant, and the Germans too directive, how on earth were the Dutch, who are far too democratic, and the Italians, too emotional, ever going to work together?

Facilitated off-site sessions with a coach enabled them to understand one thing quite clearly. 'Although we are all different, we are really all the same,' was the unanimous conclusion. The stereotypes had been masking the real difficulty, which was: 'How do we build trust in the team and learn to solve problems together?' The heated debate allowed them to recognize that there were certain things that they all wanted; everyone's blood was the same colour.

They all wanted to work with people they could trust; they all wanted to be respected and supported when they made mistakes. They all felt quite lonely quite often and having a colleague to share problems and successes with really began to energize them. They all valued and treated customers with the utmost integrity and aimed to provide world-class service. They all wanted to be successful and learn in their current roles. They were all ambitious. They were all tired from 70 and 80 hour weeks, travel and too much time away from home.

They all began to listen to one another, and understand one another better. They all learnt that placing a stereotypic perception on another: 'Oh well, of course he is English, or, of course she is Italian . . .' was not only unhealthy when communicating, but also often incorrect. A colleague who is being stubborn may simply lack confidence or feel threatened, rather than simply come from Russia.

Hiding under the umbrella of a stereotype blocks development. Being told that 'women are always emotional' will hinder a female high flyer to learn to manage her emotions. Being told that men 'never have any feelings and don't understand!' will hinder a man's ability to listen and engage with how others are feeling.

Defying the stereotypes: WL Gore & Associates in China

One of the most successful companies to overcome falling into the trap of stereotyping has been WL Gore & Associates. Tan Cher Cheng, HR Leader for the Asia-Pacific region of the manufacturer, is a Singaporean national. He tells how the organization defied conventional wisdom that you could not have a 'flat' structure with a major emphasis on empowerment and motivation in China. He took the approach that such values are universal. The organization did not ignore the legacy or the cultural nuances, but crucially took the view that they simply altered the means to the end; they didn't define everything.

'It wasn't a natural thing,' he acknowledges. 'Fundamentally, we had made a lot of effort in the selection and recruitment process. We had to pick the right people in several countries, especially in China and South Korea, who opened the door to the western world a bit later. This was not an easy task. It took a while to understand what it all meant. They naturally like what we described as our culture [but] had not totally understood it in the same way that we do. For example, we talk about an organization that's flat, with no hierarchy, and everyone is an associate; you don't have a boss. These are values that we have. A lot of people are excited, and join because of these reasons, however when on board there are times when they feel very frustrated, because they are involved in discussions, but not told what to do. It isn't a very structured process.

'"What's the right thing to do?" They ask for structure and guidance. It's a matter of education. There is a lot of guidance. We have another indigenous process: sponsorship. Every associate has a sponsor; coaching their sponsored individual. You have an opportunity to stand up and make your point. That's the idea. You have freedom to speak.

'I am Singaporean. I was involved in selection, especially in the leadership roles. We look for individuals who are very confident about themselves. They have the ability to influence strongly; people able to operate in an environment without the need to use position. Usually, we look for methods that they operate in current organizations; also their preference. There is no particular test. We are using experience; probing questions about the preferred approach. One of the basic questions I would ask: "If you were a leader at Gore, how do you think you would lead a team?" Influence, and supportive leadership, must come into it.'

It all sounds truly democratic and inspirational, but surely there is a risk that they could hire people who simply learn the talk, and turn out to be disruptive, or dictatorial underneath? How does Gore guard against that? 'Fundamentally, by reference checks; and by cross- and counter-checking questions. There are several parts of the interview. We are able to capture a 3-D view. One of the things at Gore is that most people do not see only one person in the organization at interview stage. They see 68 people, from different functions. So it's not about one individual making the decision: there is a panel, seeing them in different environments, and asking on different topics. That way we test them at different times; we should be able to get a fairly good view of the individual.

'We have a mix of manufacturing and sales in China: manufacturing at Shenzhen – in other parts there are sales operations. Over 300 are employed in China. Initially, newer associates would be given a lot of guidance and coaching. We have a "start-up" sponsor: someone who would know the associates' functional roles and business requirements. We supply a "buddy" approach to helping them.

'We did have some business leaders from other parts of Asia; from the US, Europe. We have a good mix of people starting up the process. We have a lot of operational confidence – belief in the culture itself. To have tried it out and seen it be successful is very encouraging. Initial successes made it possible, but it takes determination too. Our culture is seen as enhancing success and performance in the business. When you initially encounter challenges, you are wondering is it – the culture – helping, or is it a hindrance? For example when individuals do not understand fully what the culture means, they need to adjust their mindsets.

'When you start sharing that culture, it appears initially to be a western, American culture; but what about trust, integrity, teamwork: are they western? They're very eastern. When you get into a discussion, you find that they are universal values. Then you start moving away from the perception that it's from a particular region.'

"Values don't vary very far: it's a matter of interpretation and implementation."

This brings us back to the universality of certain values. Cher Cheng says: 'My background is organizational development. I have spent some time working with consultants, working with various organizations to implement successful corporate cultures. Usually, when you have a discussion, what values do you want your organization to embrace? There are 10 to 15 universal values. Usually, you can group all the best companies, best cultures into some core values: honesty, teamworking, trust. They don't vary very far: it's a matter of interpretation and implementation.

'When we started [in China] everyone needed a huge infusion of the culture; and now as the region continues to grow, from 200 towards 570, we continue to talk and share with associates discussions about the culture. This is also for those associates who have been around for some time, but who feel they have lost touch with it.

'The discussions on culture that I know of that we do now are done during leadership development: regular leadership meetings with associates in each location; also during business leader meetings. Usually, we have a team . . . associates attend a culture training programme. We have regular follow-ups; new associates, ask them: "How are you doing?" You ask how they are adjusting to the environment; whether they find that it's a good company to work for: if yes, why? If not, why? That will go back to the culture.'

Cher Cheng makes the point, perhaps more obvious to someone for whom English is not their first language, that the definition of the word 'culture' – a term freely bandied about in management discussions – is vague and elastic. It commonly includes national or religious connotations, but is freely used to describe the personality or way of working of a particular organization. He comments: 'English sometimes isn't as specific as we would like it to be: when we talk about "culture", we really mean "values". Many times we use the word "culture", and people think about a culture being western, Chinese or Indian. I think the culture we talk about is about those customs and ways of being brought up. It's more about values as the foundation of company culture. The *culture* in China is Chinese. The *values* of respect for each other, innovation and autonomy – which the more enlightened companies of all nations seek to nurture – are universal.'

> **❝ The *values* of respect for each other, innovation and autonomy are universal. ❞**

Culture clash based on profession

What has emerged from our interviews is the significance of a factor with which we are all familiar, but tend to ignore when discussing culture. Often the most disruptive relationships occur between *professions*, not nationalities. The conflict between software engineers, salespeople, marketers and finance people is often more destructive than cross-cultural differences.

The manager of an internet retailer, based in the USA, describes the company as follows: 'We are a company with two sides to our corporate culture. One is as a retailer. We want to be the best retailer ever. The other is as a technology company. Sometimes there is a conflict.

'We are a retailer trying to offer the best experience to customers. You have two different cultures: software developers and retailers. Retailers are very different personalities. Software engineers are more elitist. We pay them quite well.'

Allon Bloch, partner at Israel-based venture-capital firm Jerusalem Venture Partners, says: 'It's difficult to communicate, especially if you have a sales team in the US and R & D in Israel. Those people have brains that are wired differently. We try to invest in people who get the concept of working in teams, in different places. They get the fact that people are culturally different. We tend to over-communicate. A lot of time is spent communicating and managing people in different places.'

In a similar vein, Miles Flint, Global President of Sony Ericsson, says: 'If you look at sales and marketing people, irrespective of what sort of background they are from, they tend to be extroverted, while software or hardware engineers tend to be introverted. Sometimes, the conflict that you have to manage is a personality type, not a nationality.'

The internet has been constructed by software people. By and large, they are more likely to be comfortable communicating online than, say, salespeople. This is a generalization, but not a wholly inaccurate one. It may go some way to explaining the 'bullet train and the mule' patterns of development referred to in the Introduction – with the pace of change and the media for communication being set by technological inventors, not leaders or communicators, who have to struggle to catch up. It does not help that our mechanistic modelling of the company as a set of 'assets' or 'resources' artificially relegates people development and communication further down the organization.

❝Arguably there are many dimensions so 'culture'.❞ By contrast, many salespeople and executives are natural conversationalists and extroverts, who derive energy from social contact with others. So while the form of communication depends in part upon the nature of the meeting and the task, as we shall discuss in more detail in the following chapters, its effectiveness may also depend on the nature of the people taking part. For example, it may be all very well for software geeks to develop Linux online, without ever meeting, or for information geeks to keep Wikipedia up to date, but that model of communication may not be the most appropriate for getting a multinational sales team to work collaboratively on a global account.

Arguably there are many dimensions to 'culture'. Perhaps the four that are most relevant are:

1 national

2 professional

3 generational and

4 organizational.

So it could be argued that 'India', 'software engineering', 'the under-30s' and 'IBM' each possess something that we could call a culture or a personality. But the diversity within these cultures, and the threads of similarity that stretch across them, make for a complex picture, while the core needs for respect, affiliation and opportunity to learn are common to everyone.

learning points

Tips to avoid stereotyping

1 Get to know team members as individuals. Ask them about their family and interests.

2 Try to be inclusive when arranging socializing opportunities; dining is better than drinking, but be sensitive to cultural dining preferences.

3 Avoid culturally-specific topics of conversation, such as a particular sport, or the politics of a particular country which might exclude some of the group.

4 Remember that certain core needs for respect, opportunity and affiliation are common to everyone.

5 Be careful with the term 'culture'. Do not confuse culture with values; there are some human values that are universal.

6 Be aware of any historical grievances that may exist between different peoples, based on conflict, discrimination or exploitation. But do not allow people to use these as an excuse to avoid getting to know one another or treating one another with respect.

7 Similarly, be aware that prejudice against women may be a factor in creating stereotypes, and be prepared to challenge this in a respectful way. Diversity is now critical to business success.

4

Engage leadership skills: command and control doesn't work

You need to not treat employees as 19th century factory hands.

---

key points

- People thrive when working with and for great leaders. They also perform much better when they feel empowered and have autonomy. It is an apparent paradox that leaders must confront.

- Markets and technologies are constantly creating new work architecture. This makes it very difficult for managers who are 'stuck' in a model of unchanging leadership principles.

- Many leaders have been able to combine empowerment with effective processes to ensure alignment and control.

- Online communications have to be used for agreeing accountabilities and providing role clarity, as well as for information-giving.

- Leaders are learning to engage and inspire using more sophisticated enterprise mobility applications such as voice and text messages using mobile phones.

'There is a paradox at the heart of our [financial services] industry,' Stephen Brisby, Head of Investment Banking at SG, told the *Financial News* in 2001. 'On the one hand people claim they do not want to be managed, and on the other hand, if they are not well managed, they claim there is no strategic leadership.'

The paradox extends well beyond financial services companies. Indeed, this pithy quote neatly summarizes the dilemma of leadership that human beings have grappled with since the Greeks introduced democracy, and probably before. The way in which it presents itself in the modern international company is as follows: flat teams need direction, but you cannot simply order people about. This in itself is not a novel insight. But experience has taught us that under stress and pressure, many managers revert to a coercive, controlling leadership style. Thus, showing the way without 'telling' requires constant awareness and relearning. As markets, technologies and globalization change our landscape endlessly, creating certain new paradigms, a manager's duty remains to create both direction and autonomy for the team, and retain to this concept while the environment changes constantly.

Can empowerment and control live together?

As an executive in an international business you can understand advanced concepts. You can handle paradox. You may have a scientific background and be familiar with the properties of light and of electrons, that are simultaneously waves and particles. You may have an arts background, and have grappled with the Shakespearian insights into the closeness of love and death. Customers, like employees, may also face opposite directions simultaneously – for example, desiring both innovation and nostalgia.

❝The paradox in management is that people want to be free. And led.❞

The paradox in management is that people want to be free. And led.

The lesson from earlier chapters is that 'flat' teams need direction. But this cannot be effected through edicts, rules and orders. Such a course of action can be tempting. One of the companies that is most ideologically committed to empowerment and a low hierarchy is Gore-Tex and

'way ahead of the way in which we're describing companies', and that
analysis has to catch up with practice. This is supported by our own
research, which has uncovered some superb leadership and international teamwork at Sony Ericsson, Gore and
elsewhere, exhibiting practices that rarely
filter through into company reports or the
business pages. Too much business language is
dry and directionless, Lynda Gratton argues. 'This question of energy
is the new paradigm: to describe organizational forces in terms of
energy will be the next big wave.'

❝Energy is the new paradigm . . . the next big wave.❞

How do you set limits?

Key to preventing lack of discipline, while sustaining high levels of
energy and motivation, is to set limits through accountability, rather
than through rules and regulations. Andy Warrender of Gore puts a
high premium on autonomy and teamwork, but as a manufacturer the
company also has to observe strict standards of product quality and
health and safety. The company does need to have shift patterns and
strict quality control, but this does not imply 'command and control'.
It is explained under the principle of fairness – that 'you do your shift
alongside others and in keeping the commitment we have made to
customers' he says. The company makes medical products to strict
FDA [Federal Drug Administration] standards, 'so it cannot afford to
permit freedom to negatively impact our ability to live up to our quality commitment. There are rules and regulations, but these are
explained and discussed. The emphasis on explanation and involvement implies considerable effort on engagement and communication
for leaders. A challenge is not lapsing into hierarchy because it seems
easier. We keep the minimum structure. The quality standards are met,
with high levels of employee engagement; the medical products division is growing strongly and the group has never made a loss.

'We have a system in Gore of sponsorship. A sponsor is someone who
makes a commitment to help you to achieve your maximum potential
within the enterprise. A sponsor has a huge role in helping with feedback,
which is at least an annual process. He or she goes out to your peers and

gathers feedback. That gets fed back, often word for word. The sponsor would help you work through that, and help with categorizing [behaviours], for example, "You're good at such and such, but these things are not your strength". They can often tell you if you have one or two behaviours that are inhibiting you and then help you with coaching and support. I have had brilliant sponsors. People who have the confidence to tell you like it is.'

Antonio Sedan of Comai in Colombia says that leaders must only hold people to account when it really is their fault. It can seem an obvious point, but in international organizations with complex systems, it can be overlooked. He says: 'When something goes wrong, before aiming at people, I check the processes – which are the leader's responsibility. Are they suitable, well understood, and well accepted?'

The loss in terms of engagement from having too many rules can be considerable, he argues: 'Leave enough room to people to learn, think, act, and sometimes, to make mistakes. It is the only way to have people with their minds connected with the business's needs. Clear goals help.'

Jon Epstein, CEO of San Francisco-based Double Fusion, questions whether 'ending command and control' is the best way to phrase the leadership challenge. He says: 'I'm not sure that I agree with the premise. I think there does need to be a hierarchy. None of this takes away from the synergistic value of the whole group figuring everything out, but not every decision is possible by consensus. At a point, someone has to make the call and be responsible for it. You do need your colonels.'

However, his approach is not so far from that of others, as he emphasizes the importance of recruitment and of delegation to the management team. He says: 'Right now I have ten direct reports. I want to have four to five who are complete stewards of their business areas, so our conversations are about strategy – how we should pursue mobile games, for example. Even in command and control environments a lot of decisions get made that are not by the boss. There still needs to be leadership in the business overall, and the individual areas need their leaders.'

And Terry Pearce, adviser on business communication, also emphasizes the importance of discipline and accountability. He comments that as teams move to being internationally based, it is easy to overlook the importance of holding individuals to account. Online communications can be used to foster teamwork and engagement, but that's not their only use. 'You also need to hold people accountable. A mistake people make is to think only of soft things, when considering communication strategies. You also need to hold people to account. But it's easier to do that when people trust you.'

> **❝It is easy to overlook the importance of holding individuals to account.❞**

Managing the bosses: where does followership fit in?

All of us expect our bosses to manage and support us, enabling us to do our jobs effectively, and of course make sure we have fun at the same time. But how many of you ever stop to ask yourselves the question: 'What does my boss expect from me?' Not only is it difficult to manage people from different backgrounds and countries, but as 'follower' it is extremely complex to manage a boss, often bosses, on the other side of the world. Norms of behaviour, accountability, deadlines, integrity and trust work both ways.

For the millions of people who have functional and geographical reporting lines, this complexity is enhanced. Lisa, a senior software engineer currently on assignment in South Africa from the UK, comments: 'I got a few bloody noses before I realized that my functional and regional bosses didn't agree on many issues. I was dancing in treacle and struggling not to stay stuck. My US boss simply wanted the job done quickly, to meet the deadlines and with no errors. The head of Southern Africa on the other hand, who is originally from Italy, but lived in South Africa for just over ten years, wanted me to collaborate with the local team, help them upgrade their skills, not be pushy or aggressive. Meeting deadlines was simply not his priority.

> **❝I realized I needed to manage both bosses differently, otherwise I would go crazy.❞**

Being coercive and demanding with the local team in order to meet deadlines was deemed as inappropriate behaviour. I realized I needed to manage both bosses differently, otherwise I would go crazy.'

This demonstrates how followership too demands flexible and different styles, in the same manner as situational leadership.

Most managers expect their people to communicate and collaborate. Team players are sought after. They want to be able to trust them to deliver, and to receive, regular updates. They look for proactive problem solving, innovation with organizational boundaries, and people they enjoy working with. High-maintenance team members who require a lot of attention, and struggle to find the half-full glass, do not seem to progress in the flat world.

Quality of relationships, not formulae

In management, there can be a tendency to convert new insights into new rules and formulae. So, in the context of international teams, we can think 'X number of face-to-face meetings plus Y telephone conferences combined with Z hours of training on culture and empowerment means fantastic results.' There can be a reluctance to acknowledge the significance of qualitative matters. It is a game of probability, not certainty. It is important to invest in, and to be aware of, the *quality* of relationships in a team. This is the key to determining the quality of the team – and ultimately, its performance.

One cause of the reluctance to focus upon quality of relationships is that, as we have discussed, it sounds 'soft'. This is a deeply misleading metaphor. The importance of relationships is backed by hard science. There is an increasing weight of evidence supporting the importance of energy and 'flow' in individuals and business teams, and the links between these features and superior business returns. Work by Daniel Goleman on emotional intelligence and by Mihaly Csikszentmihalyi[8] on 'flow' (or personal inspiration) show the importance of individual motivation and the impact of personal interactions on performance. 'There is one member of the board who I really don't like. Whenever he starts talking I shut down and stop listening,' said one of the directors interviewed.

chairman [especially for early-stage CEO]. Often the chair is coach to the CEO, especially if the company is very demanding or it's a first-time CEO. I sit on the compensation committee; also we have the power to fire someone, so to have someone on the board as coach or friend is helpful to them. It helps them deal with the major business issues, and prepare for the board meeting.'

It is important to possess a mindset that conceives of the economic area for the business as being international: 'You have to have a global mindset – the ability to work internationally,' said one interviewee.

❝You have to have a global mindset – the ability to work internationally.❞

Jon Epstein, CEO of video games advertising firm Double Fusion, based in San Francisco, California, is recruiting worldwide as the company grows. He and his senior colleagues have spent considerable time finding the right executives for Europe and Asia-Pacific. He says: 'My experience is the following: salespeople, business development people and CEOs can all talk a good game. You have to look beyond that, and ask: "What have you accomplished?" There is a huge opportunity cost if you launch with the wrong management. Mistakes cost millions. There will be a financial cost and a reputational cost.'

❝Mistakes cost millions.❞

Jon has come to the conclusion that recruitment is just about the most important challenge that a leader has. And it has to be done rationally, on as deep an understanding as possible of the candidate, and focusing on the core skills needed – not (necessarily) command of English or personality.

In addition to the global mindset, there is the need to be comfortable in dealing with the fluid, ambiguous nature of the globalized economy. Two quotes summarize the contemporary challenge:

'I found I had hired someone who was petrified of ambiguity.'

'When I recruit now, I only want to know three things beyond experience: Firstly, can she/he deal with ambiguity? Are they adaptive and willing to learn? Do they really show respect for others at all times?'

How important is fluent English?

Capacity in English is important when it comes to recruitment, but one should not to be too swayed by this consideration. It may not be as important to the role as technical and other managerial skills, especially for individuals who are not dealing directly with customers in an Anglo-Saxon country. Jon Epstein is currently hiring in Europe and Asia as the company expands. He says: 'One thing that's interesting in Asia is: you don't want to be overly biased towards the person who speaks the best English. The manager's ability to run communication with you is important; of course you need a certain level of understanding, but whether they're thickly accented or not is not so much the point. It's easy to forget that.'

A *Harvard Business Review* article makes the same point. It reports an example of a manager setting ground rules for the team, saying that the team members 'had been chosen for their task expertise, not their fluency in English; the team was going to have to work around language problems.'[10]

Jon Epstein also emphasizes the point about avoiding jargon where possible – and not only for the benefit of non-native speakers. 'Too much business school education; too much consulting background, results in use of language that clouds the issue rather than clarifies it. "Best practice", for example. Understand what people mean by that? What should we do to stop using the phrase "best practice"? Business schools use these terms. If you're not of that background it can be obfuscating. Let's get to the meat. I'm a big believer in business process, but I want to hear it in a language that everyone understands. With some of my best employees – very bright people – I have to cut them off, and tell them to cut to the chase. I don't have time to hear all the detail; the reason I hired you as a talented individual is so that you can handle that. I have the same issue reporting to board directors. They don't want to hear every aspect of our business. Get to the nub. It sounds obvious, but people can forget it. If you're not mindful of the audience and how they process data, you can have problems. I had someone very bright giving presentations. I said: "Put it in English; adapt your communication to the audience. If you can't, use someone who can."'

The hunt for talent: recruiting via networks

Many great leaders today stay in organizations for relatively short periods of time. Databases and websites are often out of date as soon as they are updated. Networks and personal connections are now often the way to find good people. Reliance Retail in India, for example, recruited over 100 managers and subject matter experts from all over the world over a 12-month period in 2006/07. No sooner had a person received a job offer, than the first thing they were asked to do was find ten people who might be right to join the company. No headhunters were used. This has ensured that values became aligned up front, and quickly.

Taking another example, how does Jon Epstein identify business leaders? 'Unlike the stock market, past performance is the best indicator,' he says. 'We do multiple interviews – more than one interview, and more than one interviewer. Even for our lower level hires there are multiple interviews, though I may not be one of the interviewers. No one has perfect insight into communication, and we work as a team. But if the team doesn't think that there can be an effective working relationship, I give that very strong weight. I wouldn't lightly overrule a strong negative reaction. Reference checking is important and most people don't do it. I work in a closely knit industry; I know people whose names you didn't give me – you have to be careful if someone is currently employed, but even then there are ways in which you can drill down. I get a lot of calls saying that I'm listed as a referee, but I'm called to give a reference on only about 20 per cent of them. As far as we are concerned we have to get good references; you cannot get hired here without that, unless you have worked for me before.

'You have to ask the questions the right way. I'm not a big buyer of business books, but one of the most important is *Hire with Your Head*. You need the right framework for interviews; you need to do reference checking. You need to say: "I care less about your philosophy than about the projects you have worked on; how you interact with members of the team. You can tell [a lot] from the way people talk about their work and interactions with others, if you listen carefully.

Leadership is a subjective category, but good leaders have successful results. Look at the things they didn't get right and ask why. How would they change things?'

Hiring internationally introduces a whole new dimension, Jon finds. Much of the background information on the performance of a candidate is harder to obtain. 'It's harder internationally, when you're outside of the core business culture, to get at some of that information [on people's past performance]. Even between London and San Francisco work styles can be different. I know fewer people in the UK in my particular industry, so my ability to follow up and identify independently is more limited. In Slovenia I would have no ability at all. We do use search agencies. In the UK, because we are focused on people directly involved in our industry I try not to [use them so much]. Networking and references are more useful. In China, where we are also setting up, I have to use search and company financial partners. There is a lot more risk that you might not hire the right leader.'

Cynthia McCague, Senior Vice-President Human Resources at Coca-Cola, has sought to apply learning from her experience in Eastern Europe to other emerging economies such as China. What are the main lessons? 'My personal ones?' she says. 'I would say that you can never focus too much on finding, developing and retaining the best talent possible in those growth markets. It's very competitive. You develop five great people and someone will want one of them.

> **You can never focus too much on finding, developing and retaining the best talent possible.**

The other thing I learned across Eastern Europe that is applicable across Asia is that you have to unlock the wisdom in the organization. Part of what inspires people to want to be part of your team is the opportunity to make a meaningful contribution; be part of making something great.'

Another experience of start-up recruitment is that of Eric Prescott, MD of Alstom UK in the UK: 'The first thing as CEO is understanding what's the corporate direction: are you setting it or are the shareholders setting it? Once you have the direction, the plan agreed: "This is where we're going" and ask the shareholders: "Do you buy into that?"

and there is share price movement or validation. I have started enough companies, and secured buy-in from shareholders. Then it's a case of: "What skills do I need?" At Tarmac, from a three-page business plan, we created a £150m engineering business employing 4,000. I got myself a secretary. The first thing I needed to do was understand the market. I needed a market researcher, to find out: "Where is the market?" Then we looked at the segmentation of the market. At Tarmac we could do roads, structures, military installations; heavy civil engineering. There is different expertise for each of these. We identified one-off road bridges; there was a market there. You ask: "Can you serve the market?" Then you need to win the work. There is bidding time, tender time and sales time to get the tender invitations. You need someone with connections to local authorities. You need a tender team and tender manager. How do you turn a tender into a winning bid? He will then work with you and take it back to the customer. If we win this, I will make it happen. Personal relationships are really important.'

In civil engineering the demands for top technical brains are obvious, but Eric adds: 'With building a team, at each time you ask yourself: "What characteristics do I need?" I think emotional intelligence [is important]. If people are purely analytical geeks, that's OK if their relationship is only with a black box. Equally, if someone is customer-facing you have to have affability. Emotional intelligence equips you to recognize in a meeting: "I have just pushed it too far". You can watch the flicker in someone's cheek.'

One of the changes Eric has seen with globalization has been the heightened expectations of customers – corporate and the wider customer base. With companies operating in a world economy that never sleeps more flexibility is required, and this implies hiring individuals with a service mentality rather than a production-line mentality, he argues. 'We're moving towards being a service organization. Customers expect you to be there. Being a manufacturer going home at lunchtime on a Friday doesn't work any more. You need people who understand the service mentality.'

Building the right culture will attract the people you want

The most talented people want excitement, energy and opportunities to learn. Even graduates today are not always prepared to go through a two year graduate trainee programme before they get a proper job. They can access the knowledge that is freely available on the internet. Often they are more knowledgeable than their bosses. What they lack is maturity and experience: they look for a culture which will provide the opportunity to learn and acquire both.

Organizations with a positive culture and brand image have certain advantages over others. 'Top companies to work for'-type lists that have been proliferating in most major economies have become something of an industry. What emerges from these is that people are attracted to a combination of factors in which brand image, lifestyle, career opportunities and pay are melded. It also appears to be the case, though, that employers consistently misread what people want. Each year the recruitment agency Angela Mortimer conducts a European survey of client and candidate opinions. What is striking is that each time there is a huge gap between the two on the employment offering: what the candidates say they want from an employer, and what the employer offers. For the 2006 survey, 60 per cent of employers reported that their position as market leader (there is an extraordinarily high number of 'market leaders', the researchers note) would be a major attraction, but this was cited by just 30 per cent of candidates as being of any influence on their decision. The discrepancy is considerable, but understandable. The employer is proud of past achievements; the candidate is looking for opportunity. The candidates are looking to link career progression and company prospects, and many rising stars have more appeal than dominant corporate giants. This would explain why many people opt for Whole Foods rather than Wal-Mart, or for a video games start-up rather than Microsoft.

The lesson for recruiters is to try to offer individuals what they want, which may not be the same as the standard offer. The same is true when recruiting for project teams or other non-permanent team roles.

As well as considering pay and work-life balance, it is worth asking yourself: 'What role does this assignment play in the career development of the individuals I'm looking to recruit?' People can be quite long term in their thinking on this matter. They may, for example, accept an overseas posting on the basis that it enhances the possibility of being considered for a senior post a few years down the line.

The so-called 'soft' skills are critical in the flat world. Project leaders and line managers need to hire people who have heightened levels of self-awareness. The impact they have on others will either help or hinder them to get the job done. They and their team members are required to be adaptive and flexible; empathetic yet strongly focused on achieving goals and objectives; a leader at some times and a follower at others; politically aware and culturally sensitive; reflective and strategic combined with acting and executing. Values, and the ability to fit in with the culture, may make or break the team. Of course, they are expected to be bright, work long hours, hassle with work-life balance and deliver results. To cement it all, managing relationships and building trust are the foundation to success.

Concetta Lanciaux, Executive Vice President Synergies at LVMH, says: 'In any recruitment process, emotional intelligence is key. It determines whether you can work with the person. You can only judge all of these "soft" elements when you are with the person in the room. However, content, and whether you can present technical information, can be done by video-conferencing. "Soft" is not the right terminology, because in the end it's on that that you make the final decision. So it isn't soft!'

Many of these traits are difficult to gauge at the time of hiring. Assessing with psychometrics or interviews is complex. What people are asked to do in the future is often quite different from the past. The only context they have is what they did in their last job or previous company. With so much 'newness' ahead, perhaps courage and innovation stand out as desired attributes, combined with networking, and influencing. Finding this mixture is a tough assignment for any recruiter or manager.

Guiding principles for international recruitment

1 Treat recruitment as almost sacred: it is one of the most important tasks that a manager deals with.

2 Be as rigorously meritocratic as possible when testing for technical skills – use work samples; try to gauge the capacity of the individual in the day-to-day role they will actually be doing. It remains surprisingly common to test for skills that will never be used.

❝ Treat recruitment as almost sacred. ❞

3 Involve more than one individual in the hire: ideally, all the individuals who have a stake in the success of the hire. Get to know the person as a person.

4 Offer what motivates people, rather than what you think ought to motivate them.

5 Check references through networks.

6 Check for global mindset when it is an international post.

7 Ensure they are adaptive, flexible and willing to learn. Only these attitudes and behaviours will set them out as having high potential.

8 Check to prevent appointing those with prejudices and belief in stereotypes.

9 You need conceptual thinkers and innovators – plus those with the ability to work with ambiguity and fast pace of change.

10 Consider hiring for team and relationship skills as well as technical abilities, for example appoint a 'coaching' chairperson or project leader.

Part

2

The Individual

6

EQ is not enough: intelligence matters

- It is not enough just to be a 'nice person', numerical, conceptual and verbal reasoning play a significant role in being an effective leader.

- Strategic and conceptual thinking combined with strong data analysis and creating effective processes are key competencies for effective leadership. This is how strategies are decoded and business plans executed.

- Managers need to understand that organizations operate as systems, but that these systems are too complex to be described by formulae.

- Dealing with ambiguity and at the same time creating clarity for others is tough but necessary. Goals and objectives should be reviewed regularly both at a team and an individual level.

- Working in an ivory tower is not an option. Leading and managing change means that there are certain things that you can only understand and sort by actually being there.

- Understanding the history and culture of different people enables you to engage with others more effectively. Visit shopping centres, markets, and places of worship wherever you travel – it is part of the job.

- Profound changes in politics and markets do not always come accompanied by major news headlines; our antennae have to remain alert.

- Learning needs to become a continuous habit.

Management lecturer and author Henry Mintzberg delights in denouncing the Masters in Business Administration. In interviews and articles he often highlights the fact that, of the most-admired business leaders, such as Michael Dell, Bill Gates and Jack Welch, none of them has an MBA. In the examples given, two of them were college drop-outs and the other has a PhD in chemical engineering. Indeed, engineering it is a surprisingly dominant academic discipline behind successful managers. As well as Jack Welch, Tom Peters trained as an engineer first, as did Alfred Sloan of GM. W. Edwards Deming, one of history's most successful management advisers, began as an electrical engineer.

Given that leadership requires relating to people, how can this be so? One clue may be that engineering involves studying the complexity of systems. They understand that any change in one part of the system is likely to affect the whole, often in unintended and complex ways. In process control, for example, if there are just one or two variables, the maths involved is high school level, while if there are three or four, it becomes advanced calculus. Any more than that, and highly complex calculations are required to describe the dynamics involved. Sometimes, systems are too complex to be described by mathematics. Working engineers use experience, judgement and intuition far more than an outsider might expect.

Managers need to be able to apply a grasp of complexity to systems that consist of people. In this context, the variables run into the thousands, and the component parts are unpredictable sentient beings, rather than industrial chemicals or bits and bytes. So the wise manager knows that no formula will describe the reality or predict it. All this means that managers with an engineering background have several advantages in preparation for a senior post. First is a grasp of the complexity of interdependent systems. Secondly, they know that simple formulae will not work, especially where people are involved, and that experience and judgement will come into play. Thirdly, the academic grounding of applied engineering also hones and develops their thinking powers. But the systems thinking must be allied to an awareness that the organization consists of people, not parts. Deming's 14 principles of management focus at least as much upon teamwork and human fulfilment as upon process efficiency, insisting that fear is driven out of the organization, that barriers are broken down and that people should have joy in their work. These elements have not always been fully implemented in attempts to introduce Deming's ideas of quality improvement programmes.

Toyota, a company influenced by Deming and widely considered one of the best-run manufacturing companies in the world, is an interesting example. The 2006 annual report describes a significant feature of its management system: 'Senior managing directors do not focus exclusively on management. They also serve as the highest authorities in the specific operational functions. In other words, specialists have become leaders.' This system 'helps co-ordinate decision-making with actual operations'. This is similar to the blending of team and business planning described in earlier chapters. The company's new president was previously the head of its supply chain management. This would be an unusual route to get to the top in other companies. Toyota does not choose between communicator-strategists and technical specialists; rather it insists that its leaders are *both*.

> **Toyota does not choose between communicator-strategists and technical specialists; it insists its leaders are *both*.**

The ability to analyse and understand the system, and the context, remains a key attribute for the individual leader. Arguably, the importance of this is heightened as organizations and markets change so rapidly.

Intelligence matters, in both senses of the word – both in terms of mental capacity and acquired knowledge. This is not in inherent conflict with the soft skills of emotional intelligence – on the contrary, a high general intelligence equips one to learn emotionally-adept leadership skills. Traditional leadership strengths of analysis and understanding are, if anything, more in demand than ever, as technology grows in sophistication and markets change more rapidly. Emotional intelligence is fundamental to building the human internet and leading a team. But the importance of 'plain vanilla' intelligence, and knowledge of products and services, must not be overlooked.

It would be deeply damaging to create a stereotype of individuals with science and engineering backgrounds as 'geeks' incapable of relating to people. Anecdotally, we can all cite examples of engineers or programmers promoted to team leader who were poor communicators and should have stayed in a technical discipline. Equally, however, and perhaps even more damaging, has been the promotion of affable, articulate individuals who lacked technical knowledge and intellectual calibre. The research is clear. We need both types of intelligence!

The communication challenge of connecting with people across time zones and cultures through multiple media described earlier is accompanied by the equally daunting challenge of continuing to develop intellectually; to assimilate information on new technology, politics and emerging markets as well as the growing science around the human mind and human behaviour. This ability to think conceptually, deal with ambiguity as well as connect socio-economic changes with technology and consumer trends, requires strong aptitude in verbal and numerical reasoning. Your required reading may include *New Scientist* as well as the traditional staples such as *Harvard Business Review* and the *Financial Times*.

LVMH: understanding the market

Concetta Lanciaux, Executive Vice President Synergies at luxury goods group LVMH, describes how the company will study and prepare the ground carefully before setting up in a new market. Many of LVMH's brands are internationally well-regarded status symbols – Moët et Chandon Champagne; Louis Vuitton bags and so on. This does not automatically mean that the company can just sell them anywhere.

Concetta observes: 'It's important that you know the philosophy of education of the country; what the best schools are; what the local curricula are. In India, for example, if I want to hire marketing people there is no pure marketing qualification, but many engineers understand marketing because engineering training in India covers a wide spectrum. It's not like the UK, France or China. They do study the philosophy of marketing. So in India you could get a qualified engineer to be a marketer; but not in France.'

How does Concetta identify and hire the best people? 'I interview a lot of people. I have scheduled meetings with schools, with professors, with journalists and leading personalities. Over the years I studied most parts of the world to understand the specificities and imperatives of each region and brand. These are like development projects since I build on the information I gather every time. Next time there is a need I can use the previous information I have gathered.

'My visit [in autumn 2006] was in the past two months, and lasted ten days. I went with naked feet into temples, to see how people pray in the temples. It is a country full of contrasts. I saw the First Minister there, and met politicians. I met some people from investment firms, and some people in show business. My marketing manager will discover the trends and fashions. I am looking at the total cultural life. For 30 years Louis Vuitton would go into countries very early and invest for a few years. Even if we're small, that gives us knowledge.'

This depth of understanding shapes the company's business and human resources strategy, Concetta says. 'The Indian market has the potential to be the biggest, but it has characteristics that are very different from China. In China they have rejected their past; in India they love their past, and they're not ready to buy any products. Therefore you have to decide your strategy – you probably have to do a joint venture and do products with them. If you are not sensitive to culture you will miss some major opportunities. For example instead of exporting our collection, ready-to-wear, we're probably going to redesign it there [in India] with a local designer to test on the local market. In China they are very happy to buy what we're selling in America – so it's the opposite situation to India.

> **If you are not sensitive to culture you will miss some major opportunities.**

'In order to manage a Chinese operation you can have an expatriate. If you hire a Chinese person you hire someone who has not lived in China; they still don't have huge confidence in their own products. In India, it's the opposite. You cannot have an expatriate there; you will have to find an Indian, and one who has been living there. If you can't find one [with the right skills] you have to train someone from within the country – you cannot go outside of India. It is the tailor-made approach to each country. The degree of adaptation to local culture depends on how strong that culture is. There is no golden rule and every brand has to find their equilibrium.'

Alstom: building long-term connections

Eric Prescott, UK Chief Executive of Alstom (which has its headquarters in France), says that this firm also takes a long-term view to intelligence-gathering and relationship-building. 'Alstom, for example, has been in China for 80 years. They build long-term relationships. President Chirac is in China helping my group CEO pull off a big deal. The French companies build up a network over many, many years that you don't see. They sow a seed very early on. In the UK we don't do that. We believe in straightforward free trade. In parts of the developing world, Alstom is growing discreetly; it is growing relationships. They understand the value of long-term relationships; they will sit for years waiting and then will clean up, and some of their engineering products are phenomenal. They don't have an idea of cost. Concorde was a perfect example. The sheer development cost of French Government support – obliquely – that investment is huge. They sow a seed corn and wait for a long time.'

This long-term commitment to building relationships, understanding culture and understanding markets is something that can easily be overlooked in the excitement of discovery new forms of connectivity in the flat world. The very high failure rate of cross-border mergers surely reflects the understandable impatience to take advantage of rapidly emerging opportunities without paying attention to regional and organizational culture – the human internet.

> **❝In the flat world, you need to understand the nature of markets and businesses. ❞**

Sometimes you have to be patient in order to be nimble, and 'deep' in order to work 'flat'. Investment in intellectual capacity and long-term relationships remains a powerful, often hidden asset. Above all, in the flat world, you need to understand the nature of markets and businesses, as well as your own organization. In some contexts, the metaphor of 'flatness' for the global economy is unhelpful. It pertains to the electronic internet, rapidly changing markets and technologies, and ease of trade. The human internet may require depth, also.

It is not always enough to be a virtual leader

When a large chemical company lost an important customer account to a relative newcomer in the market, it woke the CEO of the chemical firm up with a jolt. He realized that he had lost an important relationship in the customer business when his counterpart had left the company seven months earlier. He berated himself for not taking the trouble to get on a plane and meet the new incumbent. When he did so a week later, he realized that holding back on travel for himself and his team had begun to have serious implications for the business. 'Virtual shouldn't mean invisible,' he told his team.

The debate about whether to travel or not reasserts itself in the context of understanding markets and customers, as well as in the context of developing teams. Some people strongly believe that you cannot understand customers or retail environments, for example, without visiting the region in which you are selling.

Jacob Aizikowitz, CEO of XMPie, reports: 'One thing that we're not doing enough is have people travelling. How do you close the gap between the R & D team and people in your team doing sales and customer support? The sales and customer support realities of whether the product is good or not – if there is praise or complaints; R & D is far away from that. They are exposed to this only if there is great praise, but they are far away from the realities, if there are problems in the market; we try to solve locally. It lands as a problem in R & D. If you don't get to a point where R & D feels the market there is a lot of frustration. I am open and encouraging to the idea of a senior engineer coming here or going to customers in Europe; to sit in the [client] organization. I encourage that. It's so that they have a better sense of what can be done. This is another example of where travel can be very important.'

And Miles Flint, Global President of Sony Ericsson, adds: 'We tend to resist cutting back on the amount of travel, because it is important that people see the factories in China [for example]. It is not at all uncommon for groups of people to fly around the world to a meeting in Beijing, [though] we also make a huge amount of use of conference calls. But we don't cut down on travel. At mid-management level the business is so interconnected that if you're trying to do something for a manufacturing operating site in China or Japan, you are needing to spend time working through the issues. It is qualitatively better than conference calls with people you don't know. At senior management level there are a relatively small number of customers around the world, you can't talk about meeting people over an audio conference. We do a day with customers and suppliers. Senior people like to meet people from handset vendors. I will do regional visits, where I will see customers. I will do retail visits; most of that can be done in two days. You cannot see how shops are laid out in Singapore unless you see it first hand; you can't get a sense of a customer without seeing them first hand.'

This understanding of markets is something instilled into executives at Coca-Cola, including the human resources function, as Senior Vice-President HR Cynthia McCague relates (see Chapter 1). The regular global HR leaders' face-to-face meeting, held two to three times a year, is at a rotating venue, so that members can combine the meeting with learning about different markets. She says: 'Last summer it was in Africa; we tend to hold these in different parts of the world. We always want to go out to the marketplace, and keep a close understanding of what's happening. This is especially important in fast-moving consumer goods companies, because markets are so diverse. It gives our people a chance to understand what's happening in different parts of the world and understand how the HR function can help drive growth in different market situations.'

Understanding the world: changes that creep up on us

The big influences upon our way of working do not come from within the organization, but from outside: technology, politics, demographics, public opinion. For an executive in an international company, some of the major events – in terms of changing the way in which we do business – from the past 20 years are:

■ The fall of the Berlin Wall.

■ The opening up of the Indian economy in 1991, with the reforms of Manmohan Singh, then Finance Minister and at the time of writing Prime Minister.

■ Industrialization and urbanization of China.

■ Completion of the world wide web in 1993.

■ Falling birth rate in western countries, combined with high birth rates in many Asian countries.

Only the first of these – the dramatic events of autumn 1989 – made headline news right around the world. To stay abreast of the others, we have to educate ourselves continually, and be aware that seemingly minor developments can become hugely influential. Not many of us will have folded the *Financial Times* back in the early 1990s after reading of the reform of India's economy and the start of the web and reflected: 'Wow! In 10 to 15 years' time India is going to be a primary source of IT and back-office services, completely transforming the way in which these services are sourced by international companies, and opening up entire regions to economic development.'

So what is going on, and why do major developments creep up on us? There is a curious dynamic in recent economic developments, that superficially appears quite paradoxical. While economists talk of the 'great moderation' – consistent growth, low inflation, high levels of investment, reductions in unemployment, this masks sometimes dramatic changes in individual sectors and supply chains. It is not the paradox that it seems, when analysed. What has happened is that the globalized economy and improved macro-economic management have between them smoothed out the highs and lows of the economic cycles.[11] All this is accompanied by considerable technological innovation. So businesses have the freedom, a degree of economic stability, plenty of cash and cheap borrowing, to enable them invest in these new technologies; and this includes new giants from China and India, often led by hungry and ambitious individuals. While inflation hovers between 'highs' of 3 per cent and 'lows' of 2 per cent, markets change with dizzying speed. At the time of writing the next in line for radical upheaval would appear to be traditional paid-for telephone connections. Voice over internet protocol (VOIP) services are on the point of reaching a scale where they can pretty much replace this traditional service. When it happens, it may happen quickly.

Wake up: the paradigm has already shifted

The flat world is ensuring that the set of assumptions, values and practices that constitutes a way of working and living is disappearing in front of our eyes. This transformation is as great as the advent of writing and then the printing press. Both transformed communication modes, the former by enabling people to record events and numbers, and the latter by facilitating the speedy transfer of information, rather than simply by story-telling. The spread of the internet and all its innovations enables people all over the globe to connect, learn and communicate – virtually for free. Fifteen years ago Second Life, Google or MySpace would have been seen almost as science fiction. Changes go far beyond simply buying goods or services online to encompass life-changing activities engaging people all over the world in marriage, online gaming, podcasting and webcams. This demands constant, ongoing change in people. The human internet has to learn how to work and live in 'interesting' times. The younger generations for the first time are often more knowledgeable, though not necessarily wiser, than their older counterparts. The flat world ensures that even any small 'Mom and Pop' shop is selling goods to anywhere in the world, that may be made from anywhere in the world. It is happening with services too; many Indian companies do online research or even online tutoring to customers on the other side of the world.

> **Fifteen years ago Second Life, Google or MySpace would have been seen as science fiction.**

Changes are radical for major companies, too. One author is working in an area going through such radical transformation, as Reliance Retail of India rolls out a programme of 5,000 retail openings in four years, establishing an infrastructure to support organized retail in many formats in the country for the first time. Most westerners regard this plan as far too ambitious. But the folks in the business don't. Indeed, the past two decades have seen dramatic change, globalizing supply and altering the balance of power between retailers and suppliers. Carrefour and Metro now operate in 25 countries and Tesco and Wal-Mart in over 12. Historically, power distribution has rested with multinational giants like Unilever, Procter & Gamble and Nestlé. Retailers, in contrast, were local and fragmented. Retailing, dominated by 'Mom and Pop' stores or national supermarket networks, was seen as an unsophisticated business, with little attention from academics or high-potential workers. The rise of giant multinational retailers has transformed the scene.

❝ The tables have turned. Manufacturers have to shift to becoming customer-centric. ❞

Typically, suppliers used to organize themselves around countries and products, utilizing their domineering power to achieve their business objectives. Today the five largest retailers account for sales of close to half of consumer packaged goods, giving retailers huge negotiating clout. The tables have turned. Manufacturers have to shift to becoming customer-centric and focus on managing relationships. This is a huge change from simply telling people what to buy and at what price.

Business leaders have to develop well-thought-out strategies for managing global accounts. Key account managers and customer team leaders, as well as CEOs, find that in order to be successful they need to meet face-to-face with their retail customers, often ceding to their demands. As retailers push strong brands and private labels to displace the weaker brands, manufacturers have had little choice but to restructure their operations in order to develop global competitive supply chains. They are desperately trying to present a single face to global customers despite multiple points of contact. Many companies such as Marks & Spencer, Macy's and Carrefour source their garments and other products through an intricate logistical dance. Manufacturing and supply chain management are now essentially borderless. Transformation of communication technologies and advanced transport methods and processes have resulted in the build-up of what only a few years ago might have been seen as an intricate, unworkable supply chain process. Many of these traders or supply chain HQs rely mainly on e-mails and telecoms as they become the search engines to find the best place in the world to buy a product. These 'traders', often based in Hong Kong, will track done the best fabrics, the best zips and buttons and other necessary bits and bobs at the best price and quality. They may also find the right manufacturers to sew these clothes, or manufacture the toys or pots and pans. Some even provide all the supply chain services to big customers such as JCPenney, ensuring that they nimbly adjust their production as required. TAL apparel makes one out of seven dresses bought in the USA, enabling stores to send them orders on a weekly basis rather than stocking up on huge costly inventories. Emergency orders can be rushed through overnight and even boxed up in separate shipments for individual stores in the large chains.

Orchestrating the supply of goods and often services (such as invoicing) between the large retailers and developing places can involve communicating with places as different as Egypt, Syria, Thailand and Indonesia, and China and South America. Central Europe is also becoming a big player in this web of transactions. It is terrifying then to note than in a poll carried out by Accenture of over 900 executives, corporate chiefs are scared that their own companies don't have what it takes to compete in this flat world. In the survey, published at the World Economic Forum in Davos in January 2007, most executives recognized that their customers and suppliers had become much more global.

❝Developing a strategy to become global and enhance the benefits of a borderless world is easy. ❞

To meet this challenge, managers and business leaders need to transform they way they build their organizations. Only if they can build a strong corporate culture, as well as understand and respect local culture, will multinationals be able to continue to grow. People have to learn to do business in countries they hardly know, aligning themselves to customs which are seemingly alien, where people around them are speaking a language in which they barely know how to say 'thank you'.

Developing a strategy to become global and enhance the benefits of a borderless world is easy. Changing the way we connect via the human internet and learning new behaviours and habits takes courage and focus.

How do we make learning continuous?

Given that we appear to have so little control over the major forces of change, what does it all mean for the individual? You are a successful business manager and might suddenly realize that what has made and kept you successful in the past might not be helpful if you are now moving into a new role or learning to manage all the dilemmas of leading and managing change in a flat world. This means understanding what your core strengths are, and aligning them to your current and future roles. Some competencies and behaviours might no longer be brought into play, but new ones might need to be developed.

The Introduction noted the importance of retaining learning from the pre-flat world, particularly on leadership and motivation, and the core principles around these skills. While certain principles are timeless, however, they may require different behaviours and strategies when applied in the flat world.

Take the case of Robert M, the Chief Finance Office of a FTSE100 company, living in the UK. He was head-hunted to be the CEO of a team to manage a private equity investment in the media industry. Not only would he get a piece of the equity, but he would be CEO at the age of 37 – a dream he had not imagined possible. The board and top team of Robert's previous company had consisted entirely of white, British men. His previous CEO had been perfectly happy for him to crunch the numbers, prepare budgets, write the annual report and talk to investors from time to time. His travel had taken him no further than Paris and Frankfurt. Imagine the transition when he was leading a team where the finance director was a Chinese woman, the IT head came from Bangalore and the head of operations was a German national. He was required to travel a huge amount, at least initially, to visit the R & D team in Israel, the IT team in India, and his key customers in the USA.

In Robert's previous organization, the culture had been very hierarchical, with a strong command and control culture. He knew the future was 'flat' in every way, but he had no idea how to get things done without being quite bossy and coercive. He realized that he was beginning to irritate his team as the chatter and laughter stopped whenever he walked into the room. Despite the fact that he knew all of this, he was puzzled as to what he needed to start doing, and what he needed to stop doing. Fortunately, Robert used his intelligence to analyse how he needed to change his behaviour, rather than to create elaborate explanations as to why he did not. He carefully wrote two boxes:

Box 1	Box 2
Stop being directive	Start listening to others
Stop expecting everyone around the world to begin and end their day on GMT	Talk to others in the early morning and late evening
Stop thinking cultural stereotypes	Respect diversity and cultural differences
Stop expecting everyone to come to London for meetings	Manage time differently
	Travel abroad at regular intervals
Stop analysing his figures	Begin to learn to manage
	Spend time on team-building and relationships

The CEO realized that this was easier said than done. Only with the help of an executive coach could he learn to unlearn to think 'us' rather than 'me' and 'I'. This was a radical change in his mindset. He struggled to drop the irrational stereotypes he had of other cultures, built into his core by education and upbringing. Only when Robert had made the paradigm shift of understanding how he was blocking the success, not only of himself, but of others as well, did he really reflect on why he was finding it tough to change. This transition to managing and leading a diverse team, with parts of the business located in far-off countries of which he knew very little, is not uncommon in our flat world. Adaptiveness needs to be genuine and sincere, otherwise people recognize that it is superficial. Unlearning and relearning is tough. Get all the coaching and support you need to make this journey.

What is noteworthy about this example is how the learning demands suddenly piled upon Robert were simultaneously about information-absorption and behavioural and cultural adaptation: the IQ and the EQ in equal measure. We need both.

❝Adaptiveness needs to be genuine and sincere.❞

learning points

How to combine strategic and conceptual thinking for effective leadership

1 It is worth considering why engineers often make effective business leaders; they understand the complexity of systems, and the limits of formulae to describe them.

2 You need intellectual capability as well as emotional intelligence to lead global teams. There is no conflict; rather the one can be used to reinforce the other.

3 Global patterns of trade and supply are changing rapidly and fundamentally, accelerated by recent benign macro-economic conditions.

4 Individual executives need to invest in continual education and re-education both to assimilate information on the global economy and to learn the leadership behaviours for managing across borders.

7

Keeping a life: questions of balance in the flat world

I am a BlackBerry widow.

There is no such thing as work-life balance, just 'work-work balance'.

---

key points

- Rising consumer expectations combined with changing markets and technology result in greater workplace pressures.
- Tele- and wireless communications mean that everyone is considered to be always contactable.
- Travel always involves an opportunity cost. Weighing the loss of either personal or main workplace time has to be rigorously assessed.
- There can be a cost to partners' relationships through long hours of work and travel, while single people face a different set of pressures.
- Quality time off, and ability to unwind, is important.
- Motivation and success have a huge bearing on whether people are concerned about work-life balance. Complaints tend to emerge when morale is low.

Labour-saving devices exhibit a curious knack of generating work. It appears to be one of the puzzles of contemporary life. The quotes at the start of this chapter show that work pressures and hours are not being alleviated in international businesses operating in the flat world. This book is not going to project an image of a largely mythical past where, supposedly, we arrived at work at nine, enjoyed long lunches and left on the dot of five o'clock. Until the early 1990s working life might have been like that for some middle-class managers in the western world. Tough economic times and serial restructuring changed all of that. Hundreds of thousands of senior people lost their jobs, and long lunches almost completely disappeared.

In addition, rising affluence combined with rising consumer expectations impacted like an ice-cold shower on workplace demands. We all started working harder and longer hours, despite transformational technology. As consumers, we want the latest, and we want it now. We want superstores to be open longer, and internet-ordered deliveries to arrive quickly. We want the latest entertainment media, broadband connections and, with the PC and laptop computers groaning under the weight of fancy software, they tend to need replacing often. So the demands upon our global organizations are considerable, and change relentlessly. We have to keep up. And we are expected to be always contactable. This goes some way to explaining the apparent puzzle that slicker technology does not necessarily alleviate the working burdens.

> **❝ We have to download our own photos now. Compile the CD. Download the music. ❞**

Even as consumers, life can become complicated. New gadgets tend to come with instruction manuals that are 70 to 80 pages long. We may have more functions than before, but the consumer is now performing many of the tasks that the supplier used to. We have to download our own photos now. Compile the CD. Download the music. We used to have people who did that for us. You don't have to be a technophobe to feel a twinge of nostalgia for a world that was simpler, if less functionally rich.

Meeting face-to-face sends a positive message

As discussed in Part 1, very few international managers feel able to dispense with international travel to attend face-to-face meetings. For every journey, there is a multi-dimensional weighing of factors to be undertaken. What will be the benefit for me and the team? What is the lost opportunity for me and the team? What is the cost to my family? The very fact of taking the trouble to visit someone sends a powerful message. Eric Prescott of Alstom observes: 'I go to Paris. You are able to persuade your French colleagues to make a decision if you go. If it's only by telephone they may put you off. They put value on the fact that I have bothered to travel. If I go to Barcelona they will realize that I'm making an investment and that therefore it's an important matter.'

Organizational culture also has an impact. WL Gore & Associates is not prepared to compromise its commitment to high levels of staff engagement, requiring a heavy investment in selection and recruitment and team development. In the multi-site Asia-Pacific region, this means considerable time spent travelling by the Regional Human Resources Leader, Tan Cher Cheng. 'We're stretched across Asia. Almost every country has an HR person there. We have an HR generalist in every country. Nine countries. One of the key things is that I travel a lot to various countries, and when I'm in those countries and working there I have opportunities to work very closely with the HR generalists there. This provides a lot of opportunities for us, on a regular basis, to be communicating. My travel time can be above 80 per cent of my time.'

A considerable amount of travel is sometimes necessary to visit markets, factories and shops as well as to meet colleagues. Miles Flint, Global President Sony Ericsson, is one such individual. There is a cost in terms of work-life balance, he acknowledges: 'My predecessor said: "You will find that never do you *not* have jet lag." It's not only typical work-life balance issues, it's working in a mode and fashion where jet lag is pretty much constant. It is immensely rewarding and exciting running a global business, but it does bring a cost, and a level of commitment that you need to make; this is a constant dilemma. I do switch off at weekends, if possible. Last year there were 26 weekends which involved travel or customer meetings. We have a place in the south-west of England where I can completely switch off, and spend time with friends who are not in the slightest interested about the company; they are interested in boating and fishing and they think I'm crazy to be doing what I'm doing. Meeting up with them is very refreshing; it gives a sense of perspective, and it's reinvigorating.'

❝You have to be in charge of technology, not allow it to be in charge of you.❞

And while it can be troublesome to be always switched on to mobile technology (and how could the Global President of Sony Ericsson not be?) conversely having a quick message to reassure you that everything is fine at work can help you switch off, he finds. 'If you get eight e-mails and four are updating you – this is what's happening – I can then switch off. It's confirmation that things are OK, and there isn't an immediate crisis. So, yes, turning it [the mobile] on sometimes is a distraction, but sometimes that 10 to 15 minutes can allow me to switch off, rather than feeling I have to reconnect the PC. You have to be in charge of technology, not allow it to be in charge of you.'

Every time you board a plane and spend hours on a flight, you are deciding not to do something else – either at work or with your family – so it is necessary that there is a clear awareness that the benefits of going outweigh the benefits of those matters that you are sacrificing. The choices are not easy, and the purpose of this chapter is not to pretend that they are, but to bring some coherence to the difficult decisions that for some people have to be made on a weekly basis.

Do we have to leave the 'real me' at the door?

Some of the tacit assumptions about management contain a quite startling contradiction. We are asked to be dedicated, naturally, putting in all the hours required to meet shareholder and customer demands. We are also expected to be rational and detached, not letting emotion cloud our commercial judgement, nor let relationships become too close (for senior executives this last edict is not even tacit, but may be explicitly defined in corporate governance rules). Devote a lot of hours, please, but leave your personality at the door by the coat-rack. There is only so much suppression or distortion of personality that we can healthily take, however, especially when asked to do so over successive 60-hour working weeks. The longer the hours, the less likely it is that we can suppress our true personalities. It is not commercially desirable either. Research by Daniel Goleman, for example, in *Emotional Intelligence*, strongly indicates that we make better decisions and are more inspiring leaders if we bring our 'full emotional intelligence' to work.[12] This demands space and time to raise our self-awareness as managers, and recognize that we continually need to adapt and change as the business world demands. Exhaustion, and stress from work overload, often cause managers to ignore the importance of interpersonal skills and good relationship management.

Some approach the whole work-life balance problem – and it *is* a problem for nearly all managers – from a totally different perspective to the usual linear assessment of hours worked. Instead of thinking in terms of hours, they think in terms of energy, motivation and quality of life. They wish to be themselves at work, a fully-balanced person. It does not present a magical solution to conflicting demands and pressures, but it does offer a more optimistic way of approaching the issue. Travel and working hours may still be longer than some would like, but the pay-off in terms of motivation and well-being is considerable, and can rub off onto the individual's family. There may, of course, still be difficulties juggling work with personal commitments and domestic life. There are approaches that can help with this (see below) but an intriguing aspect of this method is to put motivation and job satisfaction near the top of the list of priorities. No one wants their spouse or partner to be unhappy at work. Long or frequent periods away from home create their own tensions, but it is a situation many couples can work out. In some households, both work in international jobs. In other situations, the long-hours assignment is acknowledged to be for, say, a five-year period only, after which the family changes pace and spends more time together – or it might be the turn of the other partner to spend more time on their career.

David Grigson, CFO of Reuters, comments: 'I don't see travel as an interference. I don't think of work-life balance in terms of where I am or how many hours I am working; I determine my work-life balance by how motivated I feel and how energized I am. If I am travelling, but feeling very motivated and energized then I feel I have an excellent work-life balance. I know something is wrong if my motivational levels are low and I am lacking energy. I don't think of it in terms of hours worked. I don't say: "Hey, it's 8.30pm and I'm still in the office so my work-life balance must be all screwed up." Instead I say: "It's 8.30pm and if, when I finally get home, I am going to feel happy, motivated and energized then it's OK to still be here".'

> **❝I determine my work-life balance by how motivated I feel and how energized I am.❞**

Maria-Rey Marston, Executive Director at the Latin America Logistics Center, argues that the whole notion of 'work-life balance' is dated, relating to the 20th century office or factory, not the online global business environment where electronic devices combine work and leisure functions. She comments: 'Everyone does 24/7 and has a PDA. Most people do not have cut-off time, but most people don't find that a problem any more. If I'm here, deleting a chunk of mails, you may think I'm working, but I'm freeing up time, dealing with things that don't add value. There's such a blurring of work and leisure. The devices are for work and for entertainment. The new i-Phone is a PDA; it has e-mails, it's a cell phone; it's also your i-Pod for music and it has a video camera. It does video games. When people talk about separation in work-life balance, they're trying to make a distinction that's artificial. It's blurred. In the US 99 per cent of people I work with, academic and commercial people, have a home office. Maybe houses are larger there. But the first thing you do when you get home is go to the home office – then you have dinner. At the weekend, if you have a couple of hours free, you go to the home office.

> **❝I don't think the word 'balance' is the right concept. People crave flexibility.❞**

'I don't think the word "balance" is the right concept. What people crave is flexibility; the flexibility to do personal things in work time and work things in personal time. If someone works in a factory it looks like his life is balanced, but the way I look at it is that it's inflexible and unbalanced. Because if he's got to go to the kids' school on Tuesday at noon for a play he can't, the shift prevents him from doing it. And if he wants to work at home he doesn't have a laptop. So even though in terms of hours there's a clear cut-off, there's less flexibility to take a lunch off on Tuesday and catch up with e-mails on Sunday. What we crave is the flexibility to take a three-week vacation; but the price of that is you take your laptop with you.'

One practical idea is to repeat the exercise of drawing a personal network map (see page 26) – that we described for work contacts – for family and social life. Then see which areas need attention. It is perfectly reasonable to apply one's business skills to this issue and ask: in the limited time that I have, am I prioritizing time with the right people? Is it my partner, my parents, my closest friends? Might I spend more time with them and cut out an evening with new friends or a game of tennis? One can be reluctant to deploy notions of management, time planning and prioritizing to spare time, but why not? Have a 'strategy meeting' with your partner. You can always go for a romantic dinner afterwards. If your relationship with your partner has frayed, it needs repairing, and even if the meeting doesn't solve all problems, you will at least have closer understanding of each other's dilemmas and priorities. If your relationship with your partner has become seriously weakened, probably best to put on the brakes, stop reading a business book and create the time to spend together. Perhaps even take a holiday.

❝ Don't go travelling as an alternative to work. ❞ Your partner will know that with a senior job comes a heavy commitment to justify the salary. But that does not mean we should passively surrender all available time to the employer. While there will almost certainly be at least some need for some face-to-face contact with international team members, careful consideration of the right media for communication, and ensuring that the time that the team spends together is spent in the most useful way, can mean that travel is not excessive. Four times a year for a day or two seems to be a common pattern and can be perfectly adequate provided the time is used well and communication at other times is effective. Above all, as one manager put it: 'Don't go travelling as an alternative to work'. As with relationships and emotion, so with time and working hours: it's not a question of more versus less, but the right quality and the best judgement.

For individuals who are single, there may appear to be fewer problems with work-life balance, at least for those who love their work. They can put all the hours in they wish, make extra journeys, enjoy the buzz and have less need to explain unusual or excessive hours to a loved one. Such an individual is running certain risks, however. The obvious one is of physical burn out but there are other, more hidden, risk factors. Such individuals are putting a huge burden on the workplace to satisfy all their emotional and social needs, as well as intellectual and career aspirations. It feels fine if everything is going well, but what happens if the cherished project you are working on is suddenly axed? Who do you sound off to if you have had the day from hell, with a colleague making a vicious accusation, or a major client switching suppliers? There can be a certain perspective gained from discussing a workplace matter, such as a tricky decision to be taken, or speech to be made, with a spouse or someone similarly close. Alone in an apartment, problems spinning around your head can assume grand proportions, affecting judgement. So if you are unhitched, it is essential to have a bedrock of very close friends and an interest such as music, drama or sport that is completely removed from work.

It is not true to say that there aren't work-life difficulties, but it is about managing relationships, not time. In other words, instead of saying: 'I shouldn't spend more than 60 hours working this week' it is more helpful to say: 'I have these duties to these people at work and at home, where do my priorities lie?' Your daughter is due to appear in a play and wants you to attend. If it clashes with a presentation on which the future of your project hangs, you may have to say no – but really make it up to her at a different time. If it clashes with a regular phone conference that you know your deputy can handle, then going to the play will be the right option.

Do we have to have the maximum everything?

It is not only women who are encouraged to 'have it all' (top career, happy relationship, multiple happy children, gorgeous house, perfect figure). There is subtle pressure on all of us, from peers and colour supplements, to assume that one has to excel in multiple aspects of life in order to be complete. The alternative, put forward in several books and articles, is represented by extreme forms of 'downshifting', forsaking a conventional career in order to have more time in a low-cash, simple lifestyle (though the 'simplicity' of poverty is sometimes exaggerated by those who have never tried it).

There are options in between. Sometimes, making a choice, or giving something up, can be liberating. Do we have to trade up the property ladder every few years, with a bigger mortgage? Perhaps more time with the family is more precious than the extra rooms. We don't have to give up all the spinning plates and let them crash onto the floor, but giving up just one or two might be key to sorting the work-life conundrum.

❝Warren Buffet still lives in the modest house that he bought 50 years ago.❞ Warren Buffet, the second richest man in the world, donates much of his wealth to charity, and still lives in the modest house that he bought 50 years ago. In an interview with CNBC in 2007, some surprising facts emerged about the 'Sage of Omaha'. They are not related as advice; the role model would not suit all of us, by any means, and we can hardly recommend ditching cell phones and holding only annual meetings. But they are thought-provoking, all the same:

1 Buffet bought his first share at age 11 and he now regrets that he started too late!

2 He bought a small farm at age 14 with savings from delivering newspapers.

3 He still lives in the same small, three-bedroomed house in Omaha, that he bought after he got married 50 years ago. He says that he has everything he needs in that house. His house does not have a wall or a fence.

4 He drives his own car everywhere and does not have a driver or security people around him.

5 He never travels by private jet, although he owns the world's largest private jet company.

6 His company, Berkshire Hathaway, owns 63 companies. He writes only one letter each year to the CEOs of these companies, giving them goals for the year. He never holds meetings or calls them on a regular basis.

7 He has given his CEOs only two rules. Rule number 1: Do not lose any of your shareholder's money. Rule number 2: Do not forget rule number 1.

8 He does not socialize with the high society crowd. His pastime after he gets home is making himself some popcorn and watching television.

9 Bill Gates, the world's richest man, met him for the first time only five years ago. Bill Gates did not think he had anything in common with Warren Buffet, so he had scheduled his meeting for only half an hour. But when Gates met him, the meeting lasted for ten hours and Bill Gates became a devotee of Warren Buffet.

10 Warren Buffet does not carry a cell phone, nor does he have a computer on his desk.

11 His advice to young people: Stay away from credit cards and invest in yourself.

Is 'multitasking' really possible?

Linda Stone, a former executive at both Microsoft and Apple, has coined the term 'continuous partial attention' to describe a phenomenon of multiple distractions that many executives face with multi-media demands on their attention. According to a report on hr.com in January 2007, research suggests that the very word 'multitask' is a misnomer: 'There's substantial literature on how the brain handles multitasking. And basically, it doesn't . . . what's really going on is a rapid juggling among tasks rather than simultaneous processing,' Jordan Grafman, chief of the cognitive neuroscience section at the National Institute of Neurological Disorders and Stroke, USA, told the website.

Hal Pashler, a professor of psychology at the University of California, agrees with Grafman. His research has found that thoughtful actions such as decision-making must be performed one at a time. Only highly practised, automatic tasks like walking can be performed simultaneously with other actions. If workers are engaged in multiple activities at once, they're performing more slowly and less accurately than they would if they focused on each task until it was finished. 'People may think otherwise, but it's a myth. With such complicated tasks [you] will never, ever be able to overcome the inherent limitations in the brain for processing information during multitasking,' says David E. Meyer, director of the University of Michigan's Brain, Cognition and Action Laboratory. He also states: 'If you're trying to listen to someone speak while you're writing an e-mail, you might only get the gist, but not the details, of what's being said.'[13]

The implications of this insight appear subtle, but may require a profound rethink of the way in which many of us approach both our own work and the management of others' work. If multitasking doesn't really exist – it's really sequential work with frequent interruptions – we need to have a clear sense of the importance of certain tasks, and project-manage ourselves and our direct reports with great thought.

We need to place much emphasis upon the *quality* of work – just as has been noted earlier the importance of the *quality* of communication and *quality* of relationships over frequency of meeting. Often in business there is a tendency to manage against the yardsticks of numbers of tasks and hours worked, because these are the easiest to measure. It is more commercial, as well as more conducive to work-life balance, to focus instead upon accomplishments and upon quality, and to accept that some of the things that really matter are difficult to measure precisely.

❝Some of the things that really matter are difficult to measure precisely. ❞

'You get work-life balance complaints when you're losing'

Leslie Van de Walle, President Shell Retail, says that work-life balance complaints tend to be closely linked to low morale. So the quality of the working life and the achievements there are key, as well as trying to maximize control over working hours for team members as much as possible. He says: 'I don't think there are real solutions. For global teams unfortunately you cannot do that if you don't travel a lot. Unless there is a major reversal of trends, this is the reality of today's life. Are there ways of managing that? I think there are a few: one is, giving people freedom to manage time as much as you can. At the beginning, I tried all the rules: No e-mails at weekends, but for working parents it may be during the weekend that they have a bit of time [to catch up] – or when the kids are in bed. Rules don't help. The only rule is: Do what you want whenever you want as long as you deliver. I don't always expect an answer within two minutes but I do expect you to deliver. My secretary works from home 20 per cent of the time. The second one is: Use technology – once you've built up the links and the trust. A third thing is about success: You find work-life balance problems when you're losing. I work very strongly on success and recognition.'

> ❝The only rule is: Do what you want whenever you want as long as you deliver.❞

Eric Prescott of Alstom says: 'I get round it by working through the week, sacrificing myself completely, as long as I am home Friday. My wife works internationally as well. It's nothing for me to be up at 5.30. I'm picking up texts, and missed phone calls; people wanting conversations. I'm finishing about 7.30 in the evening. Then at 9.00 I'm probably in the restaurant. That means that your day gets longer. In France it is common to talk at 11 to 12 or 12 to 12.30, then they go for lunch. Our HQ in Paris has eight chefs and a restaurant that will seat 400 people. Here [in the UK] I feel guilty if I walk 100 yards to Pret A Manger. My French colleagues have a huge culture of working late [mid-week], and going home at weekends. Lunch is a two-hour break.'

There are no easy solutions for work and travel pressures and the impact they bring to bear on individual executives and their families. But excessive travel and workaholism are bad for business as well as for one's well-being, so it isn't only a question of conflicting interests. There are positive ways of approaching the issue; in particular, paying attention to general well-being and motivation, and quality of communication and relationships both in the workplace and at home.

learning points

How to improve work-life balance

1 Don't feel demoralized simply because it is difficult: in a globalized economy with high expectations of customer service, you will face hard decisions and conflicting demands.

2 Be clear about the justification and reasons for an international journey; do not undertake one unless you are clear about the benefits and make time to recover.

3 Bring your full person to the workplace. You don't need to be a different person at work to who you are at home.

4 Maintain close friends and an outside interest, even if time for these is limited. These are especially important if you are single.

5 Be prepared to deploy your management skills of discussion, goal setting and so on in your private life: discuss life and work options openly with your partner or close friends or relatives.

6 Don't let the workplace always win. It is OK to say no sometimes.

7 Be in charge of mobile technology, don't let it be in charge of you. It can be useful to set your mind at rest.

8 Remember that work-life balance is not only about hours, minutes and seconds. Quality of workplace and personal relationships matter, so do motivation and morale.

9 Don't make rules for your staff; deploy common sense and flexibility.

10 You don't have to 'have everything' – or give up everything. Be prepared to make priorities, and make choices.

11 Above all, it's about managing relationships, not managing time.

8

Ten strategies for managing in a flat world

'The hubris of science is astonishing. It will come as quite a surprise to countless poets, philosophers, theologians, humanists and mystics that complexity, diversity, interconnectedness and self-organization are either new or a science.' Dee Hock, founder of Visa.

If change is complex, and much of it sneaks up on us and takes us by surprise, are there practical strategies for living in this fluid global economy? Is there a danger of becoming so dazzled by the complexity that we end up paralyzed with indecision? Girish Paranjpe, President Finance Solutions of Wipro Technologies, based in Bangalore and operating in 38 countries, describes the challenge with the simile:

'Living in a flat world is like putting your head in the oven and your feet in the freezer.'

Change is now happening at such a pace that it takes real foresight for executives to continue to grow and adapt their leadership and work-styles as well as personal orientation to keep up. Mobility and travel is part of the job, and working with people we hardly ever see and across cultures where the values and behaviours may be very different is now an inevitability rather than a possibility. It is certainly not enough to go through a two-day workshop with a 'cultural' company to learn that Indian food may be spicy, that German mangers tend to be formal, and that women are required to cover their heads in Saudi Arabia. What is clear is that while the infrastructure and daily life in established industrialized countries has not altered much, the changes in the ways businesses have to operate are quite profound. Girish and the other interviewees do not only cope, they thrive and create great teams and great businesses. He wouldn't have it any other way. Constantly being on the go, travelling and working in different countries is exciting and makes work so much more interesting.

From their, and our, experiences, both as journalist and executive coach, ten strategies for managing in a flat world have been calibrated below. They do not comprise a simplified set of 'how-to' instructions; each one requires deep thought and ongoing commitment. The strategies are surmounted on two core themes – travel and communication – which remain stubbornly interwoven throughout.

Travel

First, travel has become part of the job. Most managers travel frequently.

How often do you make a work-related journey?

1 to 2 times a year	3 to 10 times a year	Monthly	More than once a month	More than once a week	No response
13.80%	44.80%	24.10%	10.30%	0%	7%

Communication

And secondly, all believe communication is key. Most believe that face-to-face is a must. No wonder travel is seen as a key requirement of the job.

Which means do you use to communicate with your team?

Face-to-face meetings	Video-conferences	Telephone conferences	Messenger	E-mail
96.60%	37.90%	82.80%	13.80%	96.60%

Alvin Toffler, American writer and futurist, wrote about the impact of technology in his powerful work *Future Shock*. In the 70s many of us 'poo pooed' the idea that we would all write e-mails, use mobile phones, do our shopping and banking online, and book our airtickets with a call centre based thousands of miles away. With great foresight he wrote: 'The illiterate of the 21st century will not be those who cannot read and write, but those who cannot learn, unlearn and relearn'.[14] The following strategies focus on helping us to do just that.

> **"The illiterate of the 21st century will be those who cannot learn, unlearn and relearn."**

1 Leadership style needs to become empowering and inspirational

Command and control is dead

Leadership in the flat world demands a formidable array of skills such as managing relationships, polishing up brands, fostering a culture of innovation, building up not only 'know-how' but enhancing judgement. Within this context, it must always remain at the forefront of any manager's mind that 'flat' teams have little hierarchy, and importantly, they 'won't just sort themselves out'. They need leadership and direction. This demands paying close attention to what this kind of leadership requires. Often people appear to be contrary, wanting direction and autonomy simultaneously. The effective leader sees this as a challenge, and will set a direction, then enthuse and engage people's hearts to follow. If it was ever the case that it was enough to sit behind a desk and issue edicts, it isn't now.

> *'The whole idea of a flat world is now accepted, leaders must act as a catalyst to provide the energy to help execute what is best.'*

2 A flat world means flat structures

Learn to delegate, and resist the temptation to build hierarchy

'Flat structures work best in a global setting.'

The pace of change in the flat world has killed off the centrally-controlled corporate structure. In fact, it is cumbersome, clumsy and slows down decision making, planning and execution. 'Distance implies autonomy. You cannot, as a good manager, keep a close eye on a widely-dispersed team.' This is why the issue of trust recurs again and again in teams everywhere. Managers who struggle to delegate because they believe they are perfectionists, or lack confidence to really empower others, struggle to operate in virtual teams. For many, who have worked in very structured hierarchical organizations, this transition to a different style of management often goes unacknowledged by team leaders. Influencing and collaborating are the way to get things done.

'You can only operate in the flat environment without the need to use position . . . no job titles.'

3 Recruitment of the right people makes all the difference

No longer is functional expertise or experience enough

Finding the right people for the right job at the right time can no longer simply be outsourced to HR or a headhunter. Recruitment is a fundamental, core, strategic duty of every manager. It shapes the organization. In some cases, selection for membership of a temporary project team can be as important as for a permanent post. All managers have to treat hiring as a key priority and, where possible, avoid the temptation to simply fill a post quickly, ignoring the fact that new competencies and behaviours are now required. For many positions, a combination of technical skills, relationship management, emotional intelligence and international awareness are necessary.

'People have to be able to work globally with a global mindset and understand how to work in different places. They need to like to work together. Do things together.'

4 Always show the way

Direction is critical in a flat world

'Set simple goals so that nothing is lost in translation,' one of the respondents to the online survey said. This was a consistent theme. 'Provide a simple, specific, consistent agenda with clear goals and stick to that agenda for a while, measure progress and provide regular updates,' said another. Vague or contradictory objectives couched in jargon are unhelpful but all too common in business.

Clarity of role and goals and objectives, and how they fit into the bigger picture, makes it far easier to work globally. Strong project management skills, where information about 'who is doing what, when and why' is communicated to all team members. This clarity facilitates effective working in a flat structure. As goals tend to change more frequently than in the past, the days of job descriptions that remain meaningful for more than six months at a time are over.

Leaders have to show the way by example. They are role models. Their conduct will have huge influence across the globe, whether intended or not.

'Provide a convincing and appealing vision; translate this into an achievable strategy and set of priorities and actions.'

5 Communicate often and learn to communicate well

Keeping your team well informed is not an optional extra

Virtual communications allow us to be more effective in what we do, and communicate with people we'd otherwise not be able to.

'If we have good relationships and intense virtual communications, when we meet it is like an explosion of effusiveness that creates strong bonds for the future.'

The importance of communication cannot be underestimated. It is the backbone and skeleton of every team, and every organization. Lack of transparency encourages gossip and creates mistrust.

'The biggest problem of working virtually is lack of communication. We underestimate that at middle management.'

Communication is not just about e-mails, slide presentations and video-conferences. Listening is the foundation to communication, and the biggest complaint heard in many instances is: 'They don't listen to me'. Remember, if the team have not understood the roadmap, the accountability lies with the communicator, not the people. Beware, where English is spoken well or is the mother tongue, much can still get lost in translation, simply because the assumption is 'we all understand one another'. 'The phrase "just now": in North America it has a completely different meaning to that in South Africa. For the former, it means immediately, the latter means some time soonish.'

In formal communication every medium should be used to reinforce the message. Today, leaders need to keep up with the latest technology and maximize its use. Practice and training are irreplaceable.

Informal communication is as important as formal. 'Corridor conversations are valuable, even by phone. Just *phoning* up to say: "Hi, how are you?"' Some leaders view networking and relationship management as so important that they rank informal higher than formal. Try to be available for impromptu conversations, as well.

Face-to-face meetings reinforce and enhance relationships and team effectiveness. Ensure that you make dedicated time to meet in person, even if only occasionally.

6 Teams don't just happen

Face-to-face team facilitation builds a strong foundation; focused time must be dedicated to build a team

Most managers believe that without some face-to-face contact it is very difficult to get the teamwork needed in order to manage effectively. E-mails encourage more frequent dialogue and communication, but for most they represent no way to build a team, and certainly no way to build a vision and shared goals and objectives. At the best of times it is difficult to organize and get people to work as a team to accomplish corporate goals.

Although flying is expensive and travel often exhausting, it is clear that 'teams that meet the most are the best run'. Teleconferences are seen as no substitute for 'looking into someone's eyes', seeking to understand and be understood.

7 Build trust: it is the foundation of strong teams

Get to know the team as people; help them to get to know one another

Building trust and common understanding is the cornerstone of getting people to work together effectively – more so when dealing with people from another country. They want to trust *you* first before they trust you with a major business matter.

Debate fosters trust, recognizing that other people have ideas too. Sometimes testing ideas together is a good way to start. What is clear is that trust cannot simply be conjured up. It comes from confidence and success.

In particular, be sensitive when there is a change in structure at a global level. It is seen to take up to a year to rebuild trust. People feel insecure and confused, often concerned with what seems to be loss of areas of responsibility, and insecurity about their jobs.

8 Respect cultural differences

Seek first to understand then be understood

As the team leader it is important to show your team respect – for their ideas, their knowledge and their cultural differences. After all, that is exactly what you hired them for. Show a genuine desire and ability to understand others and their culture. Pretending that cultural differences do not exist creates blind spots, resulting in a toxic culture.

'The US corporate culture is still MASSIVELY command and control. In the UK people are less respectful of authority and incredibly uncomfortable with the paternalistic model of leadership. Consequently, when the USA comes to the UK they experience people who, in their opinion, are simply disrespectful.'

In addition, the same words can have different meanings or interpretations. 'When someone in the USA says: "Do you think it would be a good idea to . . . ?" it is an order, whereas in the UK it really is a question.'

Importantly, do not underestimate the people from so-called developing countries. 'Indian IT services companies, such as Wipro, are seen as putting fear into the old guard including Accenture and IBM' (*The Economist*, 7 April 2007).

9 Work-life balance is the blessing and the curse of the flat world

Make sure you take control and make it work for you

> *'Cutting off depends on the personality of the individual, do they micromanage or do they delegate to empowered subordinates?'*

Every day millions of men and women in the workforce break millions of promises made to millions of children. They miss out on school sports days and concerts, as well as dinner with the family and bedtime stories. Having two incomes has brought economic benefits to countless families and given women rich opportunities for fulfilment. Yet now many parents are experiencing, often for the first time, the conflicting pulls of career and personal life. For some, the laptop computer works both ways: they can relax if they know things are on track, but for others, it means always being on-call. 'I have to be available 24/7. I get nervous when I am in the shower and can't hear my mobile.'

Cheerfully dealing with a myriad of commitments means being really smart about your time: 'You must let people know what your boundaries are. You need to agree these with colleagues, spouse/partner and kids, so everyone knows where they stand.'

10 Become part of the human internet

Becoming part of the flat world means enhancing your leadership skills

'Just becoming a leader that can share a vision or paint a picture of where we should be is very challenging.'

'I am constantly trying to become better at what I do.'

Many leaders today understand that emotional intelligence is 50 per cent of being part of the human internet. Thus the ability to understand the complexities of creativity and autonomy, make appropriate decisions in complex situations, adapt oneself to local businesses and cultures, combined with the capacity to have empathy, is a tough challenge. Seeing below the surface, reading between the lines is a new skill for many. In fact, some leaders deliberately focus on building an emotionally intelligent team.

Implications for boards, managers and 'ordinary' people

For people leading, managing and working in this flat world, these strategies have clear implications regarding the vision, mission, values, culture, and diversity of any business, as well as the skills and behaviours which are going to drive success in the future. What is clear is that today's and tomorrow's companies should consist of flexible and dynamic teams of enthusiastic people, who are able to work in an interdependent and collaborative fashion, with people all over the world. Such energy and direction are essential, not a 'nice to have' optional extra. On top of it all, leaders are inevitably engaged in leading and managing change.

Now that command and control style of leadership and vertical hierarchies are disappearing, managing relationships, negotiating and influencing skills have become increasingly important abilities to develop. Influencing, in particular, typically only works if people like and trust you. As one of our respondents put it: 'People are more likely to buy into your ideas if they like you.' Other points on individual leadership conduct can be summarized as follows:

Shaun Higgins, Executive Vice-President and President Europe Group at Coca-Cola Enterprises Europe, the largest bottler of Coca-Cola products in the world, has some articulate views on how leadership needs to change. 'First and foremost, it starts at the very top, at the board of directors. You need a board that is connected to the flat world, with diversity in thoughts and perspectives. Not just a token woman or board member from another country, but a board of "true equals" – equality in perspectives, that is – otherwise companies will not be able to manage globally.

'Secondly, business leaders must have, more than ever before and differently from before, the building of strategic alliances as a key component of their job description. As assets turn into liabilities overnight, the leader must be able to vision, design, build and implement strategic external alliances on all non-core capabilities with providers all over the world, working together in true partnership.'

Thirdly, Shaun believes that the leader must be, more than ever before, the chief morale officer, building an internal culture that delivers speed and scale, and rewards behaviour accordingly. 'This means speed in linking strategy to operations; scale [in] moving from [a] project in one part of the world to going pan-European or pan-Asian with a business idea that works.'

Finally Shaun believes that talent management is a very different game in this flat world. 'If the top managers all look, walk and talk the same because they have all been at the company for 15 years or more, then "mind the gap": you just might have a major disconnect with what the business is trying to do.'

So what are today's and tomorrow's successful leaders going to look like and how will we recruit them? Reliance Retail in India recruited over 15,000 people during 2006 and 2007, without the use of a recruiter or head-hunter. Each new recruit brought in ten recommended ex-colleagues or acquaintances that they thought would be a fit for the business needs. Each person is also expected to coach and mentor three people on a formal basis, as well as coach and build their own teams: quite a unique approach to talent acquisition and engagement.

Shaun Higgins is passionate about his people recruitment priorities: 'I want to recruit people for their attitude, their ability to learn and to adapt, and their skill set. The list has not changed, but the order of priority has. Skills have an ever-more limited shelf life and a closer "best before" date. People who have a can-do attitude, are full of passion and energy, who want to make a difference, who can be both good team players and team leaders. Those people will be in an ever-increasing demand. The war of talent will be about them.'

Managers should be cut from a different cloth

The traditional organization where a few top managers co-ordinate the pyramid below them is becoming a lazy dinosaur – cumbersome, clumsy and heavy. It is now time to put the best leaders in charge: relationships play as important a role as task. This will ensure that a diverse team with strong interpersonal skills will focus on collective missions and goals, take advantage of the strengths of the different team members, and know how and when to plug the gaps. Communication and relationship-building will be as important outside the teams as in them. They will understand how to dissolve silos, keep peers informed and secure engagement from colleagues for proposals and innovative thinking. They will need to build coalitions and strategic alliances externally, with government bodies, communities, vendors, and important partners. Collaboration and interdependence will be core concepts. As organizations continue to specialize there will be a greater need for teams and people to interact. The good news is that communication technologies have made this interaction much easier, and less costly.

Changing the leadership model

The way companies organize themselves and compete will have to change. Interactions like supply-chain management will tend to become increasingly complex and more multicultural. The job of a leader will be to develop a strategy whereby their teams can connect with global and often rural consumers through networks, harnessing specialized talent from anywhere that has complementary communications technology.

Leaders will have to be able to deal with ambiguity, but at the same time provide clarity to others, even if it is only on a short-term basis. An ambiguous business situation is one where the strategic and business objectives are not very clear. In fact, they may be understood by different people in different ways. The way ahead may be foggy, and in particular there may be different viewpoints about what needs to be achieved, by when and by whom. They will be required to make quick decisions very often, drawing on the valuable insights of much younger highly-skilled and highly-educated people. Judgements and decisions based on inputs of others as well as their own experience will be key. Listening and taking feedback will be essential skills. Importantly, they will need to invest time in building a culture, which will need to be embedded in deep respect for human values and cultural differences. Walking the talk will no longer be optional, neither will integrity. Only effective communication, both operational and inspirational, will ensure this happens.

Ways of being and doing

In addition to the ten strategies for managing in a flat world, here are some other imperatives for personal leadership behaviour:

- Leadership in a flat world requires leading and managing change on a constant basis. Deliberate 'change programmes' of the 1990s no longer work.

- 'Adaptive' means having to unlearn and relearn. The way you managed in the past may not work in the present or the future.

- Check the procedures and processes are right for the business; stop the blame culture.

- Observe the people around you, take time to consider their thinking and listen to their ideas. But also listen to how they feel about things, show them you care.

- Take time out for reflection and team off-sites. There should also be time for fun and for people just to 'hang out' together.

- Goal and objective setting should be clear to all. Set the guidelines but don't dictate the tactics to people; ensure empowerment within a very clear framework.
- Learn about the culture and values of others, respect the differences.
- Learn to deal with complex dilemmas. Leadership has always involved adaptability, but this has been accentuated by the rapidly changing markets of the globalized economy, and the decline of the hierarchical corporation. Strategy cannot be set in stone, and many successful companies, such as Google, deliberately build in an element of 'chaos'. Leaders have to be comfortable with ambiguity. They have to think short-term and long-term simultaneously.

Lessons from the movies

In Bollywood and Hollywood, successful directors have worked out how to hire their teams and orchestrate them to work in an interdependent and collaborative way, even if the leading man or lady is a prima donna with a big ego. They hire the best camerapeople, wardrobe specialists, lighting engineers and designers. They know that each movie or play is different, and may require a different set of skills and talents. There is always an understudy backstage, who might not seem to be as good as the star, but can shine on stage in a different way. There is constant innovation in cinema technology and stage props, people always learning from one another. Importantly, there is a seductive appeal to consumers all over the world. Tom Cruise, Judi Dench and Shilpa Shetty are household names across the globe. As leaders, managers and their teams shift in dynamic projects, team players become moving parts, often travelling around the world to build trust and connectivity.

More and more businesses are moving to this kind of endlessly adaptive and fluid model, gearing teams and allocating resources to the demands of the project or joint venture, rather than maintaining permanent institutions or silos.

Lumps and bumps in the flat world: what would make you fail?

Throughout this book leadership behaviours that are likely to ensure your continuing success have been consistently identified and highlighted. This positive focus is quite deliberate; it is now well-established psychologically that we learn best from learning positive behaviour, rather than trying to avoid negative patterns. However, this should not become an unthinking optimism, leaving one unprepared for setbacks. From time to time it is important to take stock and reflect on what it is that is going to make you fail.

From our interviews and from the experience of one of the authors as a coach (and especially in the light of her conversations with executives over the past five years as the world flattened out) there are clear themes that cause managers, leaders and organizations to struggle, and often fail. What could cause you to fail are the following blind spots:

1 Regard Asia only as a cheap alternative manufacturing base, and ignore the fact that is has become a massive and growing consumer market.

2 Burn out through stress and overwork, thinking that the heart attack will never happen to you.

3 Forget that it is your job to manage your boss. Always ensure that you build trust with them, and are aligned to their strategy and thinking. In other words: don't think it is only their job to manage you and that you don't have to be a positive member of the team and a good 'follower'.

4 Forget to spend real time, one-on-one, getting to know the people who work with and for you. This is sometimes best done informally.

5 Building a board or top team which is not multicultural and diverse. The days of the exclusively white, male, Anglo-Saxon team are over.

6 Think that it is HR's job to recruit and develop your team. It is yours.

7 Think that the only thing that matters to people is money. It is usually culture.

8 Forget that people leave their jobs mostly because of the boss. Devoting real time to understand how people think and feel about your leadership style is important.

9 Give up on visiting sites, operations and the shop floor where the real work is being done. Sitting in an ivory tower is not the way to understand if the strategy is working and how it is being executed.

10 Stick to stereotyping images of different cultures and nationalities. The people around you will soon know what you think about them.

11 Cut back too much on travel. As laborious and exhausting as it may seem, some travel is a must to building global teams.

12 Keep telling people what to do, and stop listening to what they are saying . . . not acknowledging their contribution.

Using both sides of the brain: transforming leadership

There is no doubt that globalization is flourishing, mainly because the barriers blocking cross-border commerce have dissolved. Many multinationals that have flourished over the last century now recognize the need to shed their nationalistic cultures if they are to continue to survive. The only way to do this is to take a long, hard look at what it takes to be a great manager in a flat world. Those who stick to the tried and tested ways of the past will no doubt be bruised and battered as they bang into the bumpy terrain.

The complexities of work-life balance will mean more flexible working hours, with people and teams being held accountable for deliverables and real added value rather than just hours counted at work. Only then will we learn to manage our stress, and keep fit and healthy. Performance management processes will need to be adapted to the team approach, with a focus on 360-degree feedback. 'Me' and 'I' will become 'the team' and 'we'. We will all need to become more self-aware, be prepared to acknowledge feedback, and take charge of our own learning and development, with the support of the organization we work for. With 'jobs for life' a thing of the past, finding the appropriate systems and processes to support us to work in a 'flatter' way will demand space for reflection and time out – something most of us rarely find the opportunity for. Is the real challenge 'how to live in several worlds at the same time?'

Some of these challenges are new, but some are timeless. How to deal with globalized markets, and manage teams that you rarely meet and that possess little formal hierarchy, are novel. But it is reassuring to know that the principles of communication, engagement and respect are at the heart of successful teamworking. It's the same old people in a whole new world.

Conclusion:
How to be a stand-out manager
in a flat world

In 1497 Vasco da Gama set sail around the southern cape of Africa in search of spices and other resources in the East. Just five years earlier, Christopher Columbus had more famously set off in the same pursuit but heading west, stumbling upon an entirely new continent. The principal motivation for both was establishing reliable trade routes to India and China. From one perspective, it could be seen as extraordinary that it should have taken over 500 years for these trade routes to begin to fulfil their potential, as globalization emerges from centuries of imperialism, economic under-development and protectionist ideologies. It has been a long, slow road towards the globally-connected business world that we now see emerging. For the first time since the 15th century, India and China are the principal economic focus of the West. The brain drain that affected India in particular, but also China in the latter part of the 20th century, as their economies struggled to keep pace with high educational standards, is starting to be reversed. A growing trickle of talented and successful westerners are, with rather more reliable transport and far more communication media than the intrepid explorers of the old world, looking to stake their reputations and fortunes in the East. Many Europeans in their 20s and 30s are heading to India to give their careers a kick-start. It gives them the chance to tackle something new, and learn how to work in one of the fastest-growing economies in the world. This is exaggerated by the fact that most European economies are growing by less than 3 per cent a year, and with unemployment at around 8 to 10 per cent, new jobs are sometimes hard to come by.

While most of the new expats in India are Europeans, people from the rest of Asia and North America are also sought after. In 2006 Infosys hired over 300 US graduates, mainly to have someone who understands the western customers' ways of working, at the heart of their business. Reliance Retail brought in over 60 designated 'subject matter experts' from all over the world, over a 12-month period, since the mega start-up got underway in early 2006. They came from as far afield as the USA, Singapore, South Africa, France, the UK, Argentina and Thailand with strong retail experience in some of the most successful retail chains, to take part in one of the most exciting retail transformations the decade will experience. All are thriving on the energetic pace; challenge and opportunity to play a part in something which is no longer available on their home turf, where organized retail grows at a much slower rate.

The three Cs of success in the flat world

A flat world is more than just flat structures or simply a level playing field. It is about *communicating, competing* and *collaborating* with people from many different nationalities and cultures all over the world. Most of these people are not tied down by existing infrastructure and legacy applications. Yet communication on a global scale has become a real challenge for many businesses. Understandably, CEOs are troubled as to how they and their teams will compete and commute. 'What', they ask themselves, 'can we control, and how do we build these fluid, boundaryless teams?'

Integration, bringing the personal and the corporate agendas together, is one of the key objectives in the flat world. Meetings that combine individual and team development with business goal setting are viewed as the most effective as we saw in Chapter 1.

Such integration is equally relevant at board level as well as in an operational division. This finding actually issues a challenge to the conventional way in which business is conceived and described. While globally in the pre-flat world, economies were held back by protectionist ideologies, within many corporations the brakes applied have come about through the artificial segregation of the 'people' from the company, as if they were separate. This somewhat misanthropic convention that 'people' are separate from 'the business' relegates us to being fringe participants or spectators in our own organizations. Reuniting the two is the route to success. The human internet has remained stuck as the 'mule', left far behind, as the transformation of communications climbed aboard the bullet train and sped ahead.

This book does not give all the answers to creating great international teams, but it does establish some of the key questions to ask yourself on the journey, and suggest strategies with which to approach them. The questions are:

- How do you build trust across diverse global businesses?
- How do you identify the most important business relationships?
- How do you build and sustain your own personal network when you are already working stretched hours?
- How do you manage to nourish personal relationships, and secure a balance between work and home life?
- How are you going to decide when to travel, when to meet virtually, and if virtually, through which medium?
- How are you going to combat any prejudices, or the tendency to stereotype, and show unconditional regard for others?

A new language for the flat world

So if the 'human internet' has been slow to put together compared with the electronic one, what do leaders urgently need to address? Business pages continue to be obsessed with the deals and the financial restructuring, while too much business language is passive and impersonal, talking about 'alignment' and 'positioning', rather than the energy, direction and innovation that make great businesses buzz. When performance heads south, too often there is a call for a break-up or a merger, rather than for urgent work in building teamwork and leadership. If you want an example, compare and contrast the Daimler-Chrysler catastrophe with the successes of Toyota. The merger of Daimler and Chrysler ended in abject failure on 14 May 2007, when Daimler effectively paid €500 million for Chrysler to be taken off its hands by the private equity firm Cerberus. Cultural differences and people issues had consistently been cited as posing formidable problems in the decade-long transatlantic tie-up.

Under the surface, there is some innovative and inspirational work, as the case studies in this book illustrate. These practices highlight the principles of great teamwork, while identifying strategies for coping with the inevitable challenges and frustrations. Success does not depend on nationality or organizational structure. It depends on the collective energy and inspiration harnessed by individual leaders. The research, which brings into focus the lessons and strategies for managing in a flat world, consistently highlights what really makes or breaks the business. It is the skill set and leadership behaviours possessed by individuals, and put quite succinctly, whether or not the key players actually trust one another. These aspects come to the fore even more in flat teams, which hang together solely through relationships and specialized skill sets, often without a formal hierarchy to prop them up.

Traditionally, and quite properly, managers have focused upon processes and an understanding of cost, and business structures. This is necessary, but it is not sufficient. New structures, merged companies or supply chains cannot work without high levels of engagement and trust fostered by astute leadership. Take the example of Sony Ericsson (Chapter 1). It is not by chance that this venture succeeded, while Daimler-Chrysler failed. It succeeded by planning, and by paying at least as much attention to vision, teamwork and sharing of goals and values as to strategy, planning and organizational structures. The CEO needs to be 'chief morale officer' in the memorable description by Shaun Higgins of Coca-Cola.

We need a new language to describe the reality of management and business. The 20th century lexicon of assets, alignment, hierarchy, departments and sectors is inadequate to describe the flat world or the human internet: the complexity of organizations and projects, the nuance of leadership required, the temporary and fluid nature of teams, the degree of organizational overlap, and the dynamics required for success. The ability to deal with ambiguity, combined with energy, inspiration, communication, innovation, wisdom and understanding, are what make the difference. These are the qualities that turn ordinary groups of people into outstanding teams, who trust one another, solve problems effectively, and make sound decisions. Those managers and leaders who cannot master these new leadership skills will stay stuck in the old way of doing things. They and their businesses will soon become extinct.

The heartening truth is that any group of people, from any region, nationality or culture, including a team that may stretch across the world, is capable of exhibiting these qualities. The challenges of the 'flat' world are formidable. They include the time differences, the distance, the multiple teams and the virtual meetings. But by mobilizing the intellect and energy of all members, teams can create outstanding achievements and even realize dreams.

Notes

1 Friedman, Thomas, *The World is Flat: the Globalized World in the Twenty-first Century*, Farrar, Straus and Giroux, New York, 2005.

2 Ibid.

3 In 2006 Sony Ericsson became number 3 in the mobile phones market, overtaking Samsung and LG Electronics. Its sales of €3.8 bn in the final quarter were 64 per cent up on the same period in 2005. Miles Flint said it had been an 'extraordinary year' for the joint venture. *Financial Times*, 17 January 2007.

4 In 1996, Business Process Re-engineering pioneer Michael Hammer was interviewed by the *Wall Street Journal*, which stated: 'Dr. Hammer points out a flaw: he and the other leaders of the $4.7 billion re-engineering industry forgot about people. "I wasn't smart enough about that," he says. "I was reflecting my engineering background and was insufficiently appreciative of the human dimension. I've learned that's critical."' Perhaps the deeper question is why so many executives believed, and continue to believe, that people are no more than a 'dimension' of the company.

5 Intel website 'Meet our Researchers' at http://www.intel.com/research/researchers/t_mowry.htm

6 'Totally Wireless on Campus', *USA Today*, 2 October 2006.

7 Quotes are from an interview with Lynda Gratton. See Gratton, Lynda, *Hot Spots: why some companies buzz with energy and innovation, and others don't*, FT – Prentice Hall, London, 2007.

8 Csikszentmihalyi, Mihaly, *Good Business: Leadership, Flow, and the Making of Meaning*, Penguin Books, New York, 2003.

9 Nalbantian *et al.*, *Play to Your Strengths*. McGraw Hill, New York 2004.

10 'Managing Multicultural Teams', *Harvard Business Review*, November 2006.

11 Gerard Baker, writing in *The Times* on 19 January 2007, wrote: 'The business cycle has not been abolished, but . . . it has been stretched, to improbably great lengths. In the process, the wild fluctuations of employment, output, inflation and interest rates have been firmly damped. The peaks of inflation have been lower, and the troughs of output shallower . . . The economic implications [of the great moderation] are much larger [than the political implications]. In the absence of wild swings in activity, businesses and households can plan much more easily.'

12 Goleman, Daniel, *Emotional Intelligence*, Bantam, New York, 2005.

13 Hr.com, 26 January 2007.

14 Toffler, Alvin, *Future Shock*, Bantam, New York, 1970.

Index